PRAISE FOR
MAY WE HAVE YOUR ATTI

"Feeling overwhelmed? Springboard Clinic's SELF model is a lively, approachable way to befriend your ADHD and locate the strengths that will help you thrive! If you're ready for a happier direction in your life then this workbook, and its optional workshop, are the places to start. Thank you, Springboard, for making this incredible journey of self-discovery available to all!"

—Melissa Orlov, founder of www.ADHDmarriage.com and author of award-winning *The ADHD Effect on Marriage* and *The Couple's Guide to Thriving with ADHD*

"These experienced clinicians share their strategies for building resilience, as patients struggle to find themselves in a way that moves them forward beyond their ADHD. Using characters that reflect the full spectrum of ADHD and worksheets, this book is filled with hope and a patient perspective that encompasses the full range of challenges someone with ADHD may face".

—Dr. Margaret Weiss, MD, PhD, FRCP(C), Department of Psychiatry, Cambridge Health Alliance

"*May We Have Your Attention, Please?* is a well-designed, thoughtful workbook for adults with ADHD. The authors have developed exercises to guide readers through the process of discovering and understanding their ADHD while reminding readers that they are NOT their ADHD. The chapters that help adults to identify, and lead with, strengths are an excellent reminder that we all have gifts and creativity to share with others. Professionally trained coaches can use the workbook with clients to clarify wants, needs, and the nagging 'shoulds' that get in the way, leading to a more productive and satisfying goal-setting process. I strongly recommend that the deep dive into the emotional components of the Finding yourSELF model be supported by a licensed therapist as the self-discovery process for adults with ADHD can be distressing, especially for newly diagnosed individuals and their families. Congratulations to the team at Springboard Clinic for creating a useful and engaging tool for adults with ADHD."

—Jodi Sleeper-Triplett, MCC, SCAC, BCC, Founder & CEO, JST Coaching & Training and author of *Empowering Youth with ADHD*

"This excellent guide to understanding and managing your ADHD is packed with sensible advice for patients beginning their journey on understanding ADHD. It is written by very experienced clinicians who emphasize managing the everyday challenges that our patients face. It is written in a clear jargon free style and encourages the reader to change outdated negative scripts about themselves and develop collaborative scaffolding relationships to better manage their ADHD challenges. The authors encourage the reader to recognize their strengths as well as their personal challenges with ADHD.The stories of different patient experiences provide good examples of the ways in which our patients can develop a more balanced and integrated view of themselves. The book encourages the reader to see that they are more than their ADHD.This will be a helpful book for anyone beginning to better understand ADHD".

—Dr. Laurence Jerome, MD, Adjunct Professor of Psychiatry at The University of Western Ontario

"Learning to better live with ADHD is an extraordinary journey that can lead to wonderful results when you understand why and how. *May We Have Your Attention Please?* is a toolbox that will allow you to discover different avenues on this journey—and remember to focus on the road, not the destination, which will add even more fun to the process."

—Annick Vincent MD, author of *My Brain Needs Glasses* and *My Brain Still Needs Glasses*

"This book is a gem and long overdue addition to the ADHD library, written by seasoned clinicians with compassion and good sense. Many books explain ADHD-related concepts. Some offer first-person essays, too. *May We Have Your Attention Please?* does all that—and in highly readable fashion—but then goes one better. Throughout you find abundant worksheets, thoughtfully designed to help readers sort through their individual experiences of and reactions to this highly variable syndrome. The goal throughout this guide is 'separating myself from my symptoms,' identifying strengths, and thriving in life. Five stars!"

—Gina Pera, educator, Adult ADHD expert and author of *Is It You, Me, or Adult ADD?* and *ADHD-Focused Couple Therapy: Clinical Interventions*

MAY WE HAVE YOUR ATTENTION PLEASE?

A SPRINGBOARD CLINIC WORKBOOK FOR LIVING—AND THRIVING—WITH ADULT ADHD

MAY WE HAVE YOUR ATTENTION PLEASE?

Laura MacNiven, MEd
J. Anne Bailey, PhD, CPsych

with contribution from
Dr. Ainslie Gray, MD

springboard

Toronto

Springboard Clinic
Suite 301, 1055 Yonge Street
Toronto, ON M4W 2L2
www.springboardclinic.com

ISBN 978-1-9995719-0-0 (paperback)
ISBN 978-1-9995719-1-7 (ebook)

"It is impossible for you to go on as you were before,
so you must go on as you never have."
—Cheryl Strayed

CONTENTS

We are so grateful to the amazing humans who
have supported us in the creation of this book.

Thank you to:
Lori Burwash (our editor extraordinaire),
Daughter Creative (our innovative design team),
Zoe Grams (our marketing/PR specialist),
Carra Simpson (our publishing ninja),
Krysten Cooper (for the ongoing counsel and support)
and Lauren Kouba (for believing in those notes from
the whiteboard years ago).

And to our Springboard Clinic community, both
our team and clients. We learn from you every day.
You inspire us. We love working alongside you.

INTRODUCTION

Whether you have already been diagnosed with a focusing challenge or are in the midst of asking questions about your own struggles, *May We Have Your Attention Please?* will help you understand how ADHD affects all facets of your life — and motivate you to conquer ADHD in a way that's right for you.

This book doesn't just tell you what ADHD is and isn't. We've designed it to help you ask questions about your past, make observations about how your symptoms have affected you and explore how you perceive yourself in terms of your strengths and challenges. By being more aware of your particular version of ADHD, you can approach your treatment in your own way.

At Springboard Clinic, we've been honored to work with, and be inspired by, thousands of adults living with ADHD. We have listened to our clients, heard what holds them back, learned what makes life more manageable and sat with them as they've sorted out their own identities — past, present and future. They've shown us that in facing attention issues with hope and authenticity, you can become your best self, and even leverage your brain differences.

As you work through *May We Have Your Attention Please?*, we suggest you bring yourself, your experiences and an open mind. In turn, we'll offer up our knowledge, insights and stories. Let's work together so you can understand yourself more deeply and find your way to a contented and inspired life.

Each chapter combines information about ADHD, tips to apply to your life and activities for you to complete. You'll also hear from four fictional characters — Jason, Candace, Tim and Amy. Each is impacted so differently by their ADHD, yet they all share similar themes and inspire us to see past mental health symptoms. They boldly take ownership of their personal well-being. They stumble along the way, too. You may just find yourself rooting for these fictional folks. To us, they represent resilience, growth, optimism and strength.

Feel free to doodle on the book's pages, dream in the margins and use the activities and stories to gain perspective and self-data. Skip some stories and activities and read or do some twice. We know that working through ADHD is not a linear process, but we do hope this book leads you to a place of clarity and purpose that we believe is already inside you.

WHO WE ARE →

Springboard Clinic was built on a belief that ADHD does not have to hold you back. Dr. Ainslie Gray and Laura MacNiven co-founded a small mental health clinic in downtown Toronto in 2009 with the goal of offering a space that was free of judgment and full of hope.

Since 2009, our clinical team of physicians, psychologists and coach/therapists has grown from 3 to over 20. As a team, we've evolved alongside our clients, who have inspired us to be innovative in our approaches and model of care. Our Finding yourSELF methodology pairs self-work with ADHD knowledge and expertise, in turn motivating strategic treatment and growth.

We've been touched by our clients' stories and believe that by building awareness about how your brain works (both its strengths and challenges) and accessing the right types of support, you can beat ADHD and live the life that's right for you.

LAURA MACNIVEN

I grew up not knowing I had attention issues. I didn't have obvious symptoms, and there was little awareness about non-hyperactive types of ADHD, both in my home and in our health community. I learned how to compensate, but I often did things last minute. My report cards frequently said, "If she tried harder, her results would be better."

The pieces started to come together when I was an adult. And as I saw myself in ADHD, I became passionate about learning as much as I could about attention issues and the brain and began to develop supports, both for myself and for those who had similar challenges (and gifts). My personal experiences with attention issues fueled the development of the Finding yourSELF program.

I'm an enthusiastic, creative and compassionate leader who likes to geek out on topics like curriculum development and spiritual growth. I could not be more excited to share this book with you.

In my spare time, you'll find me hiking, writing, hanging with my two children and husband or on a run with my giant dog, Fifer.

DR. ANNE BAILEY

I always knew I wanted to work in a field helping people, but it took a little while to find the right area. Like many of the individuals I work with, I had several interests growing up — music, sports and dance, to name a few. I completed an undergraduate degree in physics and geophysics, but in my last year changed my mind and introduced a minor in business management. I then took a year off to figure out what I wanted to do and ended up falling in love with psychology. From there, I didn't stop until I completed my doctorate in psychology, studying the impact of musical training on the brain.

About five years ago, I stumbled into the world of ADHD at Springboard. My work here allows me to teach people about their brain and support them as they make changes in their lives. There's never a dull moment at our clinic, and it is such a pleasure to be so closely involved in people's life journeys.

I should mention that I'm not the workaholic type. I enjoy spending time with my husband and daughter, cooking, eating out, walking around the city of Toronto and being with friends and extended family.

DR. AINSLIE GRAY (AUTHOR OF CHAPTER 9)

I've been passionate about and immersed in the medical world of ADHD support for over 20 years. A family doctor by training, I was challenged by patients with learning issues and mental health diagnoses and realized how responsive to treatment this area of medicine could be — for both the patients and the support team. I became empowered and passionate working with ADHD patients and their families. With the availability of new pharmaceutical agents and the collaboration and skills of diverse healthcare professionals, this area of psychiatry has changed dramatically.

Springboard Clinic provides services for comprehensive care across a person's lifespan, fulfilling a professional dream of mine. Through my personal experience with attention issues, I've been able to connect deeply with the patients I see and share a much-needed message of hope.

In my spare time, you will find me swimming, being a grandmother, meeting new friends everywhere and embracing life challenges as they come.

THIS IS LAURA

(YOU MET HER ON PAGE 4)

Dear reader,

Welcome. Welcome from the bottom of my heart. This book is the result of my own experience of coming to terms with my attention issues — the Finding yourSELF journey it walks you through has changed my life. I hope it will catalyze a powerful experience for you too.

Before you start, take a breath, give yourself a pat on the back and find somewhere chill to reflect on the journey ahead. You might be feeling super motivated and ready to fly through the upcoming pages — that's great! But it's also okay to take small steps. You're already taking a big first step just by beginning the process of learning about your brain in the context of ADHD.

However you're feeling, I want to share some thoughts:

Take this book at your own pace, and in your own order. You don't need to do it front to back. You don't even need to do the whole thing. This book is jam-packed with information, tools and techniques, so flip through and decide where you want to start. Maybe you want to read all the characters' stories first, or try an activity that jumps out at you. You can do it in pieces or from cover to cover. Find your way — it's all okay.

Be kind to yourself. This book has the potential to impact how you think about who you are. It asks you to dig deep while exploring stuff that might be layered, emotional and, at times, difficult. Give yourself space to reflect, ponder and apply what you've learned in a way that works for you. Most importantly, go easy on yourself.

Reach out for support. You're not alone. If you're struggling — even if you're not — don't hesitate to seek out medical or psychological help.

If you'd like help with staying accountable and feeling connected, check out Springboard Clinic's online course. This workshop-style group program will assist you as you work through the Finding yourSELF model in this book. For more information, visit springboardclinic.com.

Finally, you'll be hearing from me, Coach Laura, a lot. Personally, I love being called a coach — it feels right for me. However, many of the techniques I discuss are a blend of therapy and coaching that step outside "coaching" guidelines. So if you're working through this process with an ADHD coach, explore with them whether there are issues that are better addressed with a registered therapist.

Now, let's get started!

— Coach Laura

CHAPTER 1

THE FINDING YOURSELF MODEL

At Springboard Clinic, we learned early on how important it is for you to own your journey. In too many instances, mental health diagnoses and treatments can feel "top-down" and more like the clinician's view than your own. We believe you are the expert of your world, and the Finding yourSELF model will help you assess who you are and what symptoms you experience and then build solutions that work for you.

Before we get into the actual stages of the Finding yourSELF model, let's examine how we define attention issues because, you see, "Attention-Deficit/Hyperactivity Disorder" doesn't really explain the root of the problem. It explains that you struggle with symptoms of inattention, hyperactivity and/or impulsivity more than the average person. But what do you do with this information? Give in to a reality where you just can't regulate your focus? Where you passively stand by while ADHD controls your life and identity? We don't think so. Let's take control and be informed.

Technically, there are three types of ADHD based on the *Diagnostic and Statistical Manual of Mental Disorders, Fifth Edition*: predominantly inattentive presentation, predominantly hyperactive/impulsive presentation and combined presentation. A list of symptoms helps clinicians identify which type of presentation of ADHD an individual meets criteria for.

Generally speaking, inattentive type tends to be symptoms that are categorized as inner restlessness, while hyperactive/impulsive often shows more visibly to others, with more symptoms of outward restlessness. The combined type is for individuals who struggle with both groupings of symptoms. Despite the different outward manifestations, all are a manifestation of the same brain difference (trouble regulating your ability to focus).

Attention issues are on a spectrum. Like depression, anxiety and many other mental health disorders, you can have mild to severe symptoms of ADHD. What is happening in your life or what you are trying to accomplish can make symptoms improve or worsen and can also make the impact of symptoms more evident. So, the severity of symptoms is individual, but also depends on environmental factors, life stressors and daily demands or responsibilities.

Once you understand that ADHD is something you can take control of, learn to work with and even master, you can start the process of healing, strategizing and believing in a better life for yourself.

"So it's not something that will make me a total failure?" Not at all.
In fact,

learning how to master your ADHD brain can put you in a position of advantage.

We're not saying it's easy, and we definitely agree it can be unbelievably exhausting. But there's good news: ADHD often offers people the ability to access "hyper-focusing," easily think and see outside the box and find solutions where others are stumped. To get there, you'll need to do a few things, which this workbook will help you with: learn how to let down your defenses, admit where you struggle and put strategies and support systems in place, all while sorting out where you fit in.

That's where the Finding yourSELF model comes in — it helps you understand different pieces of your assessment and treatment journey. It is about you, about harnessing your strengths, coming to terms with your weaknesses, learning how to take responsibility for symptoms and maybe even learning to laugh at your quirks. This process involves separating yourself from your symptoms to help encourage and empower yourself in all aspects of your life.

S → SEPARATING YOU FROM YOUR SYMPTOMS

E → EVALUATING HOW YOUR SYMPTOMS HAVE IMPACTED YOUR WELL-BEING

L → LEARNING HOW TO MAKE CHANGES FOR THE BETTER

F → FRESH START TOWARD A NEW PHASE OF CONTROL

To complete the Finding yourSELF methodology, you will work through these seven stages, chapter by chapter:

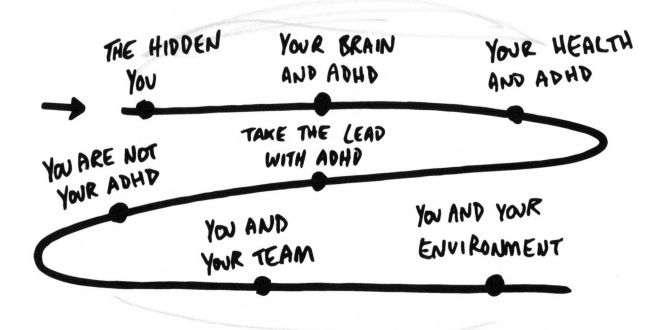

THE HIDDEN YOU

YOUR BRAIN AND ADHD

YOUR HEALTH AND ADHD

TAKE THE LEAD WITH ADHD

YOU ARE NOT YOUR ADHD

YOU AND YOUR TEAM

YOU AND YOUR ENVIRONMENT

We hope these stages will help you process where you have come from and start to believe in a future where more of your intentions are put into action, where you can set individual limitations, start building sustainable habits and work toward a place of peace and joy. So many of our clients have found their way using the Finding yourSELF model, and we believe you will too.

It takes a lot of courage to seek help for mental health symptoms. And when you do open yourself, a diagnosis should bring answers to questions you've been trying to understand and put you in a position to move forward. There are, of course, no easy fixes — having ADHD is daunting, frustrating and bewildering. You may have longstanding disappointments or feelings of anger. Even if you do feel hopeful, you may be afraid of letting yourself or others down.

Now it's time to meet our friends: Jason, Candace, Tim and Amy. Imagine you're in a group program with these four. Connect with them, disagree with them or wonder alongside them. Their stories are meant to give you company, make you feel less alone, as you work through each chapter.

These fictional folks are not intended to be a full representation of ADHD, nor do they represent groups or the entire population. They do, however, share familiar stories we've heard from our clients over the years. So don't be surprised if you find yourself relating to these group members — that's the whole point.

JASON

Jason is 21 and has a personality like a "tornado," a name he earned when he was a local football star. Jason lives big and loves big. In fact, everything about Jason is big: his personality, his body, his voice. His booming laughter brings joy and energy to his family and friends. He has a way of reading situations, cheering for all those around him. He's one of the most well-liked individuals in his community.

Jason had a couple secrets though. He always struggled with his schoolwork and became self-conscious about his body and eating habits. Despite his outward confidence and popularity, he hid feelings of shame about his struggles.

During his first year of university, Jason was unable to keep up with the pressure he felt to be the life of the party and to be so much to so many. As things worsened, he was drinking almost daily and binge eating. Although he was trying to find control in his life, he felt like it was impossible to live up to what others expected of him.

It all snowballed quickly. After suffering through an episode of depression during finals, failing too many first- and second-year courses and drinking more nights than not, Jason was sent home from university.

Grasping for answers and feeling uncertain about how he had let everything that mattered to him go, he reached for mental health support and was diagnosed with ADHD, the combined presentation. For a guy who cared so much, Jason was lost. "Everything I touch turns to mud," he said. "Every time I try to pick myself up, I fall harder the next time."

Finding out that ADHD was at the heart of his struggles was partially a relief, but it also stirred up a lot of anger. To Jason, it seemed like too little too late. He'd already let everyone down, and it felt like the mountain ahead was too big and too steep to tackle. How could he face those who had such hopes for him? How could he ever get back to the place where he was? How could he ever go back to school?

The guy who'd had so much promise suddenly found himself in his parents' basement, feeling like he'd been hit by a truck.

Like many adults we meet, Jason would need to go backward before he could move into his next phase. To find his own way — and a new way of being and living with ADHD — he'd have to shut down the imagined critical voices of others and see for himself where everything had gone wrong. He had to ask himself, "Am I really a tornado, or have my symptoms made me that way?"

Candace

Candace is 36 and has an important job at a software design firm. Carefully put together, she is similarly gentle, slow and careful with her thoughts and words. You wouldn't have any idea she struggles with inattention, social anxiety and often negative thoughts about herself. A reliable, diligent team member, Candace works long hours, often immersing herself in projects as a way to avoid situations that make her anxious outside of work. Throughout her life, Candace has walked away from relationships when they started to feel serious and has been unable to be intimate with romantic interests.

Candace would never have guessed she had ADHD, the predominantly inattentive presentation. Having grown accustomed to the constant scattered thoughts in her mind, she thought everyone felt that way. She coped using different defense mechanisms and makeshift strategies and had no concept of living and feeling any other way. It wasn't until her eight-year-old niece, Zoe, was diagnosed that she started to put the pieces together. Like Candace, Zoe was bright and talented but struggled with many of the symptoms she experienced.

When Candace finally made the connection and was diagnosed with ADHD at 35, it all started to make sense. She'd been a debilitatingly shy child. Afraid of birthday parties, field trips, new people and most foods, she struggled to sleep on her own and constantly hid in her interests.

With her vivid imagination and bright intellect, she coped by immersing herself in her passion: video game design. Candace created narratives for characters and spent a great deal of energy focused on her own creative pursuits. By the age of 12, she'd made her own robot. By 15, she'd designed her own video game. During her teenage years, she would have to fight back tears when things didn't go as expected or when plans changed. She mostly kept to herself and struggled with her scattered mind and "black and white" thinking in social situations.

As Candace reflected on her life, she realized that the way she saw the world was not the same way others did. She began the slow process of "letting go" and giving in, with the goal of finding a place of peace in her own mind and gaining more self-confidence.

Candace's journey required her to dive deep into the layers of her past, particularly around her fears and feelings of anxiety, in order to open herself to her community.

Tim is a 45-year-old lawyer with a wife and two children. He comes across as polished and poised, always immaculately dressed. But by the time Jane, his wife, had convinced him to get assessed for attention symptoms, a few years ago, his marriage was in tatters and he had grown distant from his social community.

It had reached the point where Tim and Jane were constantly fighting. Tim was drinking more and was rarely home for dinner, claiming he needed to work late. Always quick with an excuse, he was essentially emotionally unavailable to his family and fixated on his own needs. He would zone out when people talked to him, his mind wandering, particularly in conversations with Jane. She wanted him to be more involved with household tasks and parenting in general, but then was critical and impatient when he made an effort. He felt like he couldn't win. By the time she gave him an ultimatum to get help, they were both exhausted and hopeless. In fierce denial, he blamed everyone else.

It would seem unlikely that, as a lawyer, Tim could struggle with attentional issues. He'd always been a high achiever and had everything going for him on paper. Well known at his firm for his attention to detail, he was often the first one at the office and the last one to leave. But by the time he sought help, he was totally burned out. No longer able to put in the same extra-long hours, he was having trouble keeping up with his workload.

As Tim became more honest with himself, the signs were easier to identify — they were all there. Unknown to his coworkers, he'd always struggled to focus to get his work done and frequently had to pull all-nighters to meet deadlines. If people rushed him or called him out on his forgetfulness, he became stressed or overwhelmed. His whole life, Tim had carried around this sense of being an imposter, which made him feel disconnected from others, despite his outward confidence.

When Tim received a diagnosis of ADHD, predominantly inattentive presentation, he was surprised and somewhat in disbelief. In a million years, he never would have guessed this to be a possibility. Distant, angry, defensive and completely exhausted, he had a long way to go before he could see the light at the end of the tunnel. Tim's journey would include a hard look at himself as he learned to forgive his actions and find his true self. To make the necessary changes in his life, he would have to work toward awareness and acceptance.

Amy is 47 years old. She has a loving, supportive husband whom she married soon after high school. Together they have three children. She is active, energetic, talkative and works really hard to do it all. Despite this, Amy has struggled with periods of low mood as far back as she can remember. It was not until her adult ADHD diagnosis that she understood why her life had gone the way it had.

As a child, Amy felt she was smart, but thought teachers never liked her. They seemed to be annoyed when she talked in class or blurted out answers. She even remembers a teacher taping her mouth shut in grade three to "help" her pay attention and not disrupt the class. Amy enjoyed playing sports and was on numerous teams in high school. She never really liked school though and didn't go to college or university. Instead, she started working right away, as a waitress, an administrative assistant and finally as a certified personal trainer. She loved working with people and being active. Her clients liked her too, and she got them results. Amy had trouble with the scheduling part though and sometimes mixed up appointment times. After her third child, she decided to stay at home with her children instead of returning to work.

At home too, scheduling became stressful for Amy as her children grew up and got involved in activities and school. She would forget some of the kids' activities, the house was a mess more often than not, and their meals were usually last-minute based on what was in the fridge or on the take-out menu.

Amy wasn't feeling like herself. She didn't enjoy her day-to-day life or what her life had become in general. She felt little enthusiasm for running the household and supporting her children's needs. She couldn't do the activities she once enjoyed and had even started to lose interest in things that used to make her smile. She was crying almost daily and losing her sense of identity. Eventually she stopped making the effort to see friends or get out of the house.

At that point, with her husband's support, Amy went for a psychological assessment. She was diagnosed with depression as well as ADHD, the combined presentation. While she wasn't surprised about the depression diagnosis, Amy didn't know anything about ADHD. At first, she didn't believe it, but decided to look into it and learn more about what this meant for herself and her family.

That decision would be the key to unlocking her spinning life, stepping off the rollercoaster and helping Amy understand why things had become what they had.

CHAPTER 2:

THE HIDDEN YOU

To understand how you are being affected by attention challenges, think about who you are at your core. By finding your true self — your identity, strengths and values — you can create a vision of how you want to live your life. This means becoming more aware of your wants and needs and listening to that voice inside you, the one that knows about your true self, the one you have probably quieted over the years as you've struggled to meet expectations, the one that will show itself if you give it a chance.

ADHD does not have to define you.

It's simply a term to describe a set of symptoms. This first step in your treatment journey is about starting to believe there's something greater beneath and beyond your symptoms. This step is also about breathing, reflecting with yourself and having faith that there are truths inside you that will help you customize your process. This is not about self-critique. Quite the opposite, this is about looking inward, free of judgment.

Dr. Ross Greene, an American child psychologist and author, has shown us that how you approach managing ADHD symptoms is vital to the outcome. He explains it in the context of parents and teachers when it comes to children with ADHD. When we consider a child with ADHD who is not meeting expectations, there are two main philosophies: either the child is not doing well because they don't want to, or the child is not doing well because they can't.

The philosophy a person subscribes to determines how they handle a situation when working toward a desired outcome. If the parent or teacher believes a child will do well if they want to, their approach will be different than if they think a child needs help or skills development to succeed.

WHAT IS MY PHILOSOPHY ABOUT MY ADHD?

The pivotal first step of your journey is understanding your personal philosophy about your ADHD symptoms. To do this, apply Dr. Greene's concept to your individual situation.

Pick two areas in your life related to ADHD where you're not meeting your own expectations and write them in the top two boxes. For example, maybe you struggle to be "in the moment" with your partner, can't stay on top of healthy eating or aren't productive enough at work. Answering these questions will help you better understand your internal dialogue.

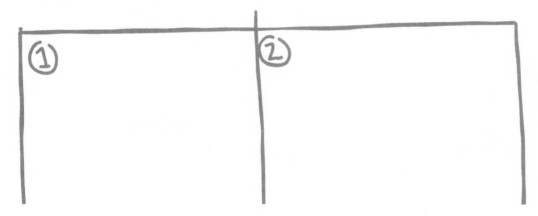

1. Is it because I don't know how to do this well or because I have lost the motivation to keep trying? Or somewhere in between? Jot down whatever comes to mind.

2. Can I do better at this if I try harder? Or am I struggling with symptoms and/or skills deficits? In other words, do I need help?

3. Are my intentions in the right place, but things somehow don't work out the way I want? Or am I giving up before I get started?

4. Do I think I'll have success simply by trying harder, or do I need to reframe the situation to try differently?

NOW THINK ABOUT YOUR OWN HEADSPACE AND START FORMING YOUR PERSONAL PHILOSOPHY ABOUT YOUR ADHD SYMPTOMS. DESCRIBE YOUR SYMPTOMS AND HOW THEY IMPACT YOUR EVERYDAY LIFE.

We know this is a broad question. Write whatever comes to mind!

How you conceptualize and make sense of your symptoms affects how you approach your treatment process overall. It determines your voice and your approach for change. It is pivotal to assess who you are in relation to your diagnosis. If you (or those around you) believe you're not meeting expectations because you "don't want to," well, this is very different than if you believe it's because you "can't."

The "don't want tos" can become very damaging in relationships. For example, imagine a husband who's *always* late for dinner and *always* forgets his wife's birthday. There are two interpretations of this behavior: he doesn't care enough about these things *or* his ADHD symptoms impact his time awareness, attention to detail and ability to remember events. If his wife reminds herself that these things are unintentional and her husband shows his love in different ways, the damage can be lessened.

Actions, or inactions, can be interpreted through the lens of empathy instead of anger. These differing interpretations drastically influence how we respond to situations where symptoms of ADHD are at play.

A STORY FROM COACH LAURA:
WHY THE PHILOSOPHY MATTERS

I remember the first time I worked with a teenage client who fundamentally believed she was lazy. This idea was cemented when her parents came in telling us just how "lazy" she was. What was so interesting to me was how it had become a character judgment, and the more entrenched they all became in this belief, the more difficult it would be for her to challenge this judgment or make changes. The more everyone named it as a character flaw, the further we would get from positive change.

I could see they all wanted the same thing: for her to feel more empowered to reach her goals and dreams. But as long as they stayed in this headspace, there would be no possibility she would get to where she wanted to go, and her motivation to prove she wasn't "lazy" would dwindle.

One day, I looked this young woman in the eyes and said, "I don't believe you're lazy. I don't think you're someone who lies on a couch and doesn't care about anyone or anything. I really don't think that's who you are. What would you say if I suggested that, instead, you have trouble starting tasks? That when you go to start a task, you get so overwhelmed, experience feelings of self-doubt, get distracted, don't know where to start and get blocked by cognitive challenges and then resort to feeling like you're lazy? What if your brain is shutting off before you can even give it a real try?"

It wasn't an answer, it was a question. And from this perspective, we began a new dialogue that allowed her to start to figure out who she was and what she wanted. We explored the root and the layers to help sort out where she wanted to go. She worked to find her hidden self.

WHEN YOU WERE DIAGNOSED WITH ADHD HOW DID THAT CHANGE THE WAY YOU SAW YOUR PAST SELF?

In this section, we want you to view your symptoms differently, which will allow you to begin separating out your true self. We want to guide you to go backward before going forward, because how you feel about where you've been matters and affects how you see yourself now.

Let's first understand how a diagnosis of ADHD can change the way you look at your past. Especially for those who aren't diagnosed until adulthood, ADHD becomes an all-encompassing explanation for why their life has gone the way it has. Allow yourself to look at your history through a new lens.

How did our group members respond to their diagnosis?

JASON: For me, not to be too dramatic, but it was earth-shattering. On one hand, I was relieved because it made sense and I'd been struggling to live a certain way for a long time. I was so focused on everyone else that it felt like I finally had an answer. On the other hand, I had no idea who I was or where I fit in. If I wasn't the "tornado," who was I?

I had to go back and look at my history to sort out how things had gotten so far out of line. Honestly, it's been hard. I had to look in the mirror and reconcile the different me's. My past self, although popular and successful, would have to step aside as I worked to find out who the real me was. No longer was it about what everyone else thought — it became about me.

CANDACE: I think I first made a connection between how anxious I was all the time and my symptoms of inattention. There were so many things I thought I didn't like, or had assumed were just part of my personality, but I realized they were actually about avoiding feeling anxious. I'd told myself I was happiest at home alone. I'd written off so many things in my life.

When I got diagnosed, I asked myself how much ADHD has led to anxiety and avoidance in my life. With this lens, my whole history came into view in a new way and I started to want more for myself and to figure out who I wanted to be outside of anxiety and ADHD.

TIM: Well, at first, I didn't buy it. I'd gone to law school and didn't think people who did well at school could have ADHD. But over time, little things kept popping up that explained a lot. The diagnosis gave me some answers about why I always had to put in so much extra time and effort to do well.

I'd missed out on so much as a result. I realized I'd probably never really been present with those around me — all this time, Jane had been commenting on it and I thought she was being overly sensitive. I mean, whose wife doesn't feel ignored? My entire life, I'd been going through the motions at home and at work, not realizing I was always trying to compensate for how I struggled inside. That was hard to accept and made me feel both sad and angry, to be honest. I couldn't see a way to get out of the rut I was in — the rut I'd always been in.

Considering the past with an ADHD lens made me rethink the way my future could look. I realized how I didn't want to be anymore and started to imagine the changes that could improve my life. That part felt empowering.

AMY: Oh, I was annoyed that this was another thing I had to deal with and learn about. Honestly, I was so tired. But when I began learning about adult ADHD, especially in women, so much of my past made sense! All those years in school, I thought I wasn't trying hard enough or wasn't smart enough, but learning that it wasn't totally my fault or even in my control was a real game-changer.

I kept picturing my little self muddling along and — this might sound crazy — but I wanted to go back in time, give myself a hug and say, "Stop trying to do everything for everyone. You'll find your path." I mean, that's honestly how I reacted.

It took me a long time to accept that I couldn't go back and rewrite all those difficult moments and that that little person was still inside me! I had a lot more life to live. I guess for a while I mourned my past. Then, at some point, I felt ready to find the Amy in me, outside of ADHD, and to rebuild my life with this knowledge.

After getting a diagnosis of ADHD, it is helpful to view your past experiences and struggles through an ADHD lens. In processing what your diagnosis means, you may experience different feelings: relief to have some sort of explanation, sadness about lost time, frustration it wasn't handled differently when you were younger or validation to learn that others share similar challenges. Ideally, you'll also experience hope that this information will lead to a new phase of your life with a stronger sense of control.

There is no right or wrong way to look back on your past with an ADHD lens.

See what comes up for you as you work your way through the next two activities.

REVISITING MY PAST

Write a letter to yourself at a pivotal point in your past. Perhaps you are eight years old and starting to have challenges in school, or heading off to university, or beginning a new stage in your career. Speak to your past self with an awareness of what you now know, and think about what it would have meant to know this information then.

Be gentle. The goal here is to find clues about your true self, outside of ADHD, that will guide you along your journey.

DEAR

WHAT IF I HAD KNOWN EARLIER?

If I had been diagnosed when I was younger ...

WHAT MIGHT HAVE BEEN DIFFERENT?	HOW DO I FEEL ABOUT THAT?
ARE THERE ANY ACTIONS I CAN TAKE NOW TO HELP SETTLE THESE FEELINGS?	AM I READY TO MAKE PEACE WITH THIS?

Tip from Coach Laura: *Don't worry if you can't let go yet and find yourself holding on to ghosts from the past. You will get there — it's a process.*

HOW DID CHANGING THE WAY YOU SEE YOUR PAST SELF HELP YOUR PROCESS?

Once you're able to look at your past through an ADHD lens, you'll be able to chart a course forward. Let's see how that readjustment helped our group members.

JASON: I started to find a place of forgiveness and took my first step toward giving myself a break. It was like, there's actually a reason for why my life has been spinning out of control. Instead of looking at my past through such a critical lens, I began to feel some compassion.

CANDACE: Thinking about my past, I saw this zigzag pathway of avoidance from one thing that scared me to another. I sometimes think in "video game" terms, and I could literally picture this lost, layered, smart, well-intentioned person sleepwalking through life. By realizing that this was how I was living, I was able to make a mental shift. It's how I have come to be who I am now.

TIM: Can I say I think my past self was a jerk? (ha) No, actually, I'm sympathetic to my old self. I feel sorry for how many walls I'd built up — I was a bundle of negative coping mechanisms. The hardest part is thinking about what type of father I would still be if I'd never figured this out. Forgiving my past self has been huge. I can't believe how different I feel and *am* now.

AMY: I guess things just started to fall in place. I saw my past self as going from one crisis to the next, running around like a chicken with her head cut off. Now, I can sit in who I am. Understanding who I am and why I've been the way I have has been so illuminating. It's allowed me to step away from the spinning and start breathing.

As you consider the impact of ADHD on your past self, does anything come into clearer focus for you? How do you imagine that shifting your perspective could change how you move forward?

AS YOU STARTED TO UNDERSTAND MORE ABOUT YOUR TRUE SELF WHAT DID YOU REALIZE ABOUT YOUR PRESENT SELF?

You've thought about your past and how a diagnosis of ADHD affects how you make sense of it. What about your present self? How do you feel about how you spend your time and what you value in your day-to-day life? Does the way you're living your life feel right for you? Before you explore this question for yourself, let's see how our group members answered it.

JASON: I started to understand that I wanted to be *me*, not the me others thought I should be. I know that sounds cheesy. But, really, at one point my ADHD coach asked me to write down any moments where I *didn't* feel anxiety or pressure. At first, I couldn't find a single moment. That's how bad it had become.

For days, I just kept thinking how not okay I felt. But one night I was walking my dog and throwing sticks in the park when it hit me: "I'm okay right now. In this moment, I feel okay." I walked home and told my parents I didn't want to play football anymore and I was going to walk the dog every day for the next 30 days. It was funny to them — so out of nowhere. But for me it was the beginning of my journey to finding my true self.

CANDACE: After I'd taken time to come to terms with all the things I'd been missing out on, I wanted a do-over. My anxiety around doing things was still there, but now I had this overwhelming motivation. I wanted to have all these experiences I'd been avoiding. I wanted to go camping and finally take swimming lessons. I wanted to take my niece Zoe to her dance class. I felt like the world could open up for me.

I knew I'd still have moments where I crashed and burned, but now I was willing to take the risk of looking foolish and have faith I could figure out how to handle these situations. Basically, I decided I wanted a real life. Even if it was going to have lows, I was determined to take risks and put myself out there.

TIM: Once I'd moved past the frustration and sadness, I was able to look around me. I was struggling most with being in the moment and had kind of decided to start by faking it until I was making it, or something like that.

Turns out, my kids were my greatest teachers. One day, I came home on time, for once, had dinner with my family and then blurted out to Jane, "I'll do bedtime tonight." I knew exactly why she was looking at me with disbelief. My 10-year-old son looked at me, then at her, and then the words, "Awesome, Dad, I have a great Star Wars book." He brought me back to the present. Tears welled up in my eyes. He was giving me another chance.

In that moment, I knew I'd missed out on so much. But in his words, I also saw a glimmer of hope that I could repair things. I could do bedtime tonight, and that was a start. As I walked up the stairs with my kids, I looked back at Jane and her eyes softened. Maybe things were going to be okay. Oh, and the book was awesome!

AMY: I had to stop lying to myself. That was the biggest thing. I was running in circles, doing everything and nothing, and my days were racing by. As a mother of three kids, I was busy of course, but I wasn't as stuck as I thought.

I realized that if I was going to take care of anyone else, I had to take care of myself. That meant learning how to breathe, sleep, get exercise — and stop being so hard on myself. I had to figure out how to work with my ADHD to get all the household stuff done at least to the point where nothing was a disaster, without beating myself up. I had to figure out the difference between wants, needs and shoulds, and I had to learn a *lot* about gratitude.

Looking back allowed me to see my old life through a new lens and find alignment between who I used to be and that life I was living. One of the best things I learned was the power of mindfulness as I moved through my days.

TAKING STOCK OF MY PRESENT

Explore how you feel in your current place. As you complete these statements, do your best to put away those pesky feelings of self-doubt and step away from the voices of others.

I describe myself as …

I am not …

I care about …

I want to spend more time in my life on …

I have always thought I would …

I feel most at peace when …

I feel most frustrated when …

I wish I had more _____ in my life.

When I've had a day with parts that feel "good," what were those good parts?

When I picture a perfect "me" day, it involves …

I feel most settled when I am …

AS YOU STARTED TO ENVISION YOUR FUTURE, WHAT DID YOU WANT MORE OR LESS OF?

You've thought about your past and asked yourself challenging questions about your present. Now imagine what a more genuine and peaceful future looks like for you. First, let's see what that looks like for our friends.

JASON: Overall I wanted more quiet, less noise. Funny that I'd been called "the tornado" my whole life, when all I wanted was more time with my dog and space to return to school with a less social and more supportive scene.

I felt really minimalist about everything. I wanted to feel more accepted even if I wasn't doing the most exciting things. I reached out to a few close friends and they were so great. I realized they didn't expect what I thought they expected of me. I was still me, just a more relaxed version.

I started coming out of a fog and envisioned a future filled with stuff that was productive and meant something. I decided to go back to school and work toward a degree in social work. My favorite thing? I started volunteering with kids at a center for underprivileged families. Helping others and feeling appreciated were what I really needed and wanted.

CANDACE: My biggest realization was that I wanted to find intimacy in my relationships. That meant I needed to reduce my distractions with the next big new thing. I had to learn to be at peace when I was around others, too. Not worry so much about whether I was paying attention enough or saying the right thing at the right time. Honestly, though, I really wanted to have a romantic relationship. So, to answer the question, I wanted more connection, less distance. I think that sums it up.

TIM: Sometimes I have a nightmare I'm back to where I was, distant and moving through life in my own self-absorbed bubble. It scares the living daylights out of me. My future? My answer is simple: more play, less work, more time with my family, less focus on money and success.

AMY: I have a lot of hopes and dreams again. I want to get back into personal training but focused on mental health and busy moms. I'm still a mom of three, so everything is a bit crazy, but I feel different inside, I guess.

I want more "being nice to myself" and more "letting go." I want to go to bed at a reasonable hour and stop writing thank you notes to everyone and their dog. I want less trying to do everything, and instead do fewer things with more attention and care. It sounds simple, but it's a whole new world to me.

It's time to rejoin the group with your answer to the question,

AS YOU STARTED TO UNDERSTAND MORE ABOUT YOUR TRUE SELF WHAT DID YOU REALIZE ABOUT YOUR PRESENT SELF?

MY ENJOYABLE DAY

Now it's your turn to envision what you'd like your life to look like. Start by building a picture of what an enjoyable, manageable day looks like, feels like. We don't mean the kind of day where you're chilling on a beach or burning up the ski hill. We mean a normal day that also feels good.

Explore what you value and prioritize. Maybe you want to look for your keys less and meditate more. Or spend less time on your phone and more time being kind to yourself. Whatever it is, be honest and specific. This is the beginning of your blueprint for change. By starting in a micro way, you'll see how small goals can improve your everyday experience.

Time	How I'd spend it ...	How I'd feel ...	How is this different from my days now?
Morning			
Midday			
Evening			

MY FUTURE SELF

When it comes to feelings and actions, what do you want more of and less of in your future? At this stage in your life, with your knowledge about ADHD, what matters most to you?

FEELINGS		ACTIONS		PRIORITIES
Less of this	**More of this**	**Less of this**	**More of this**	**What really matters**

WHAT DOES MY MIRACLE LOOK LIKE?

In our coaching, we often use a version of the Miracle Question approach, inspired by Solution-Focused Brief Therapy developed by Steve de Shazer and Insoo Kim Berg.

When our clients aren't sure where to begin with making changes, we have them tease out a starting point by pondering the Miracle Question: If you woke up tomorrow morning and a miracle had happened while you were sleeping, what things would be better for you?

Consider what that "miracle" looks like for you. What would be the first thing you'd notice? What would be different? Which of your "problems" would be solved? Do you simply wish you'd have a tidier apartment, or that you and your daughter actually talked to each other? Jot down your thoughts.

WHAT HAVE YOU LEARNED IN THIS CHAPTER?
WHAT DO YOU NOW KNOW ABOUT THE HIDDEN YOU?

CHAPTER 3:

YOUR BRAIN AND ADHD

Neuroscience is a fascinating field, but a large gap still exists between the research world and the techniques people can use to improve their day-to-day functioning. Humans are variable, studies are not perfect, and many steps are involved in analyzing brain-imaging results. Keep that in mind when making sense of the latest findings, but understanding the basics of how your brain works can help you feel more empowered and motivated when working through your ADHD symptoms.

There are two main parts of the brain that will help you understand your experiences.

The first, at the front of the brain, is the *prefrontal cortex*.

Sometimes referred to as the "conductor" for the rest of the brain, the prefrontal cortex is associated with a set of cognitive skills called executive functions. It coordinates all the cognitive skills involved in *executing* tasks on a daily basis from start to finish, accurately and efficiently.

Planning, organizing ideas, getting started, prioritizing, managing emotional reactions, sustaining attention and inhibiting impulses are some of the functions it controls.

The prefrontal cortex is the last part of the brain to mature, developing until our mid-20s (if not later for some), so you may have noticed that you've become better at these things as you've gotten older. (At least compared to when you were a teenager!)

The other relevant brain system is the *limbic system*, which is deeper in the brain.

Its structures are involved in motivation, emotions like fear and pleasure, long-term memories and learning. It plays a pivotal role in sending messages to the rest of the brain about basic survival needs, like fight-or-flight responses or caring for and bonding with our young.

While early studies in neuroscience focused on anatomy and structure, newer techniques are allowing for the study of the brain at a systemic or network level. The prefrontal cortex and limbic system work together to help us get through our days and tackle our tasks. What this means is that how we react at an emotional level to situations and the contextual factors we experience influences our ability to access the skills required to execute tasks.

"Wait, if the limbic system talks to the prefrontal cortex, does that mean how I feel about something makes a difference in how I am able to use my brain?"

Yes, _exactly_.

If you feel afraid of a test, or you're worried about being overwhelmed or bored at something, this will affect how your "conductor" operates in a given task. You may be getting blocked before you even start. In contrast, when you're motivated by or passionate about something, you may be getting stronger signals, which explains how you're able to succeed better in those circumstances.

Think about the effect the prefrontal cortex and limbic system have on you. ADHD is not just conceptualized as inattention or hyperactivity. People with ADHD tend to report difficulties *consistently* accessing their executive functions, as well as managing their emotions and forming or recalling memories (for example, "Did I actually lock the door?").

One theory is that the neurotransmitter molecules responsible for communication operate differently in an ADHD brain, particularly in the areas of the prefrontal cortex and limbic system. When someone has ADHD, they have a neurotransmitter molecule imbalance, making sending messages and staying engaged, at times, unreliable. Why this happens still remains largely unknown, but we do know ADHD is hereditary and is also affected by your environment.

To support the challenges of ADHD and improve the functioning of the prefrontal cortex and limbic system, medications have been designed to change the brain's neurotransmitter balance. (For more on medications, see chapter 9.) But you can do other things to help improve brain function and manage your ADHD symptoms, independent of medications.

As humans, we have this wonderful ability to self-reflect and introduce changes to our daily lives that can improve our situations and leave us feeling more in control. So, in essence, the power is in you.

HOW DID UNDERSTANDING HOW YOUR BRAIN WORKS INFLUENCE YOUR APPROACH?

Once you know more about how the prefrontal cortex and limbic system work together, you can outsmart your brain. Let's see what our group members discovered.

JASON: It was weird to learn about the ways my brain worked and didn't work. I always kind of felt like everything was up to me and my choices. I never really thought about *not* being the life of the party — I'd just always been that way. But when you start to understand how the brain works, you realize there's so much going on up there!

Realizing this made me see how fast I was always moving. It felt really out of control. If I was running on autopilot all the time on speed mode, it probably meant there were ways to slow things down and make different choices. I could take on the driving — and change the course, too.

CANDACE: It's easier to explain this from the negative perspective. There are certain situations when my brain kind of seizes or stops working. I don't always notice it in the moment, although I'm getting better at that. But it's like it stalls and I can feel my conductor falling asleep. The opposite happens, too. When I'm fired up, I can get complex tasks done at an incredible rate. In those moments, I almost get a "high" as I'm able to access exactly what I need and it pours out of me.

I just find the ups and downs so exhausting. It's draining whether I am under-focusing or over-focusing. Now that I know what's happening in my brain, I try to work on deep breathing and being more aware. But it's hard to go from one extreme to another all the time.

TIM: When I learned what the prefrontal cortex is supposed to do, I immediately thought, *Those are ALL the things that are hard for me*. I remember hearing the list — starting tasks, staying on task, blocking out distractions, working memory, regulating emotions — and feeling like the psychologist was reading from a list customized for me. It was so weird to have someone describe my struggles so specifically. It was also somewhat relieving to understand that it wasn't a matter of me being lazy ... all this is happening at a neurobiological level.

AMY: It's funny, you only ever really know your way of doing things, so when I started learning about the prefrontal cortex and the limbic system, I realized that lots of people have different ways of getting things done and going about their days. Like, my natural state is bouncing from one thing to the next and back again. Somehow I make my way through things, but it was really important for me to understand *how* I go about trying to get things done. It's made a big difference in how I motivate myself to tackle the family calendar, the laundry and especially meals and groceries.

Another optimistic and empowering phenomenon in neuroscience is neuroplasticity — the idea that our brains are not fixed, that neuronal networks and brain structure may change based on our experiences and how we spend our time. In other words, it's never too late to learn new tricks.

This adaptability is so important to keep in mind when trying to manage ADHD symptoms or learn new habits. Many people with ADHD have such a longstanding history of difficulties that they might not be aware of how their brain has developed since they were a child. But until you understand how your brain works, it's hard to take control and change the way you live your life. With ADHD, your brain might be operating off old habits.

Now it's time for you to take control and learn new tricks.

Tip from Coach Laura: *Working with client after client with ADHD, I see shared cognitive patterns. One I've called "getting upset about being upset." They would be upset about a situation — like being late or disappointing someone they cared about — but as we explored their feelings, we realized the bigger problem was their own reactive headspace.*

The problem wasn't so much the tardiness or disappointment, but how emotionally paralyzed they would get, stalled in feelings of guilt and shame. They were so upset about the situation, and so frustrated with themselves, that they couldn't get out of this headspace and access what they needed to fix the problem.

If you catch yourself being upset about being upset, take a moment and separate the situation from its corresponding pattern of knock-on effects. What is the real issue? This can be a pivotal step in the right direction. It's more easily said than done, but at least for many, naming their response can help.

UNDERSTANDING YOUR SYMPTOMS DEEPLY

In chapter 2, we encouraged you to think about who you are away from the symptoms you experience. We wanted you to think about your true identity, independent of your symptoms of ADHD. We wanted you to do that so you could explore your voice, and any feelings that might be masked by your diagnosis.

Now, as we start to focus on the symptoms of ADHD, remember what you've learned about yourself. As you go through the process of understanding your symptoms, you can work to a place where you can have control over your future wants and needs.

As we discussed in chapter 1, ADHD is a neurodevelopmental disorder with three types: predominantly inattentive presentation, predominantly hyperactive/impulsive presentation and combined presentation. There are nine inattentive symptoms and nine hyperactive or impulsive symptoms. The combined presentation applies to individuals who demonstrate both inattentive and hyperactive/impulsive symptoms.

GETTING TO KNOW MY SYMPTOMS OF ADHD

To better understand which symptoms most affect you, check the ones that are present for you and give an example of a situation where they play a part. This activity is not meant to diagnose you with a particular type of ADHD, but to help you learn how these symptoms impact your life. (We've adapted these from the *Diagnostic and Statistical Manual of Mental Disorders, Fifth Edition*.)

Symptom of inattention	Is this present?	Sample situation
I have challenges with attention to detail or make careless mistakes.		
I have difficulty sustaining my attention on tasks.		
I often do not seem to be listening when spoken to directly.		
I have difficulty following through on instructions or completing tasks.		
I have difficulty organizing tasks and activities.		
I avoid, dislike or am reluctant to engage in tasks that require sustained mental effort.		
I lose things necessary for tasks or activities.		
I'm often easily distracted by extraneous stimuli.		
I'm often forgetful in daily activities.		

Symptom of hyperactivity/impulsivity	Is this present?	Sample situation
I often fidget or tap my hands or feet or squirm in my seat.		
I leave my seat in situations when remaining seated is expected.		
I run about or climb in situations where it is inappropriate.		
I'm unable to engage in leisure activities quietly.		
I'm often "on the go," acting as if "driven by a motor."		
I talk excessively.		
I often blurt out answers before the question has been completed.		
I have difficulty waiting my turn.		
I often interrupt or intrude on others.		

Tip from Dr. Anne: *This activity is not the whole picture because you are a biased rater! If you're up for getting a different perspective, ask someone who knows you well to complete this ... you might be surprised at the results. It can be freeing to realize that others don't notice what you notice in yourself, but it can also be eye-opening to hear what people notice that you might be ignoring or trying to stay blissfully unaware of.*

Despite attention and impulsivity being at the heart of ADHD, almost all individuals with ADHD struggle with accessing their executive functions *consistently*. Remember that conductor and the executive functions?

Let's talk more about those executive functions. This term refers to a group of skills or abilities that we all use every day to respond to demands placed on us, plan out our days, make decisions, complete tasks efficiently, regulate our emotions and act in ways that align with our intentions and values.

People with an ADHD-style brain go through their days exerting a lot of effort willing themselves to use their executive functions. You planned to, but forgot. You tried, but gave up or ran out of time. You got yourself in front of your computer ready to work, but then spent four hours on the internet and lost track of time or stared at the blank screen, unable to get started.

WHICH EXECUTIVE FUNCTIONS ARE RUINING MY INTENTIONS?

Reflect on which executive functions are challenging for you, and provide examples of how they get in the way of your best intentions.

We've adapted the functions listed on the next page from BRIEF®: Behavior Rating Inventory of Executive Function, by Gerard Gioia, Peter Isquith, Steven Guy and Lauren Kenworthy.

Executive function	Is this hard for me?			Example
	Yes	No	Some-times	
Inhibiting impulses				
Shifting between tasks				
Controlling emotions				
Self-monitoring				
Initiating				
Working memory				
Plan/organizing				
Monitoring tasks				
Organizing materials				

Tip from Dr. Anne: *Sometimes you experience symptoms of ADHD because you actually have ADHD. Other times, the symptoms can be the result of other mental health issues. For example, if you experience anxiety or depression, you may struggle to complete tasks or follow through on goals in multiple contexts. You may have difficulty with all the tasks in the chart above. If you are unsure of the root of your struggles, seek medical or psychological support.*

IF YOU HAD AN ADHD BIRD, WHAT WOULD IT LOOK LIKE?

It can be helpful to actually name the nagging symptoms and feelings of doubt that pop into your brain. By giving an image to that voice of ADHD, you can separate your own wants and needs in your internal dialogue. For example, picture a parrot sitting on your shoulder saying things like "You don't need to leave yet, traffic won't be bad" or "You'll go to the gym later" or "Wait till the last minute, that's when you get your best work done."

ADHD BiRD ↑

TALKING BACK TO MY ADHD BIRD

In becoming aware of your thoughts and feelings about your goals, successes and frustrations, you can stop ADHD symptoms in their tracks. By talking back to your "ADHD bird" and learning how to outsmart it, you can change cognitive patterns and avoid getting stuck in the same pitfalls. Notice how your symptoms nag at you and try to be a step ahead!

SEPARATING MYSELF FROM MY SYMPTOMS

Now that you have the understanding and the language to reinterpret your experiences, put them to practice. Jot down a few sample situations that routinely challenge you, along with your usual interpretation of them. Then unpack them with your new understanding of executive functions and ADHD symptoms. We've done one to get you started.

SITUATION	MY USUAL INTERPRETATION	MY REINTERPRETATION
- Running late for ... anything really	- Why does this keep happening to me? - Maybe I don't care enough about this? - People might think I'm rude or that I don't think this is important. - Next time, I will leave earlier.	- I have trouble planning, estimating and keeping track of time. - I get easily distracted or caught up in things. - I can be forgetful (even with things that are important to me).

WHEN HAVE YOUR ADHD SYMPTOMS ACTUALLY COME IN HANDY?

We've focused a lot so far on the challenges ADHD symptoms present, but they can also be a benefit, your strength, a help. In fact, there are times when you might actually hyper-focus, be productive, really engage with a task and perform well. We refer to this as the "ADHD stars aligning." These stars tend to align during highly rewarding or stimulating activities, when there is urgency, in high-stakes scenarios or when there is novelty to the activity or situation.

Let's hear what our group members say about how their ADHD symptoms have helped them.

JASON: Oh, I can still turn on my "life of the party" self when I need to! I can talk to anyone, get to know anyone. What's weird is I find it rejuvenating, not tiring (when I'm on, at least). I can go go go in social situations — other people have said they can't keep up with me. I think it comes in handy when I really want to leave an impression. I guess I'm not easily forgettable.

CANDACE: I've learned that the way I connect the dots and make associations is a gift. I come up with ideas that help my game designs. Although, sometimes they're so out there, I need to run them by someone else to make sure they're not too out there. I can also learn and retain a lot about topics that interest me, which comes in handy in my industry. It's a weird combination of knowing the business world, predicting trends and bridging the communication gap with the technology behind it all.

TIM: When I have a really big deal to work through and the stakes are high, I can feel the difference in my productivity and the way I think. I come alive. I get a boost from knowing I'm under pressure — I've always been like that. I can problem-solve, analyze and see things in a way that others might not.

 **AMY:** Whenever people are counting on me, I rise to the occasion. It's much easier to get going and find the motivation when I'm taking care of someone else. It might be at the last minute, but it always gets done. My energy keeps me going and helps me get lots accomplished in a day — friends comment on my energy levels with envy. Oh and whenever I'm on vacation or traveling, I get this buzz that feels so great — it's exhilarating being out of my everyday life!

Now it's your turn. When has ADHD worked in your favor? It might be hard for you to see the advantages at first, but, trust us, there are some. Think of when you've thought outside the box or noticed things others hadn't. We've yet to meet a client who hasn't experienced some advantages that come with an ADHD-style brain!

Tip from Coach Laura: One ADHD "gift" many clients have talked about is when their mind suddenly comes together in a way that almost feels like a superpower. Maybe it's an intuition about how people are feeling or the ability to crank out something at the last minute. They become "unblocked," able to seamlessly move through the task from start to finish.

As you learn more about how your brain works and the situations that help you engage focus, leverage that knowledge. You can almost "trick" your brain into those "lightning bolt" moments by choosing tasks accordingly.

WHICH SITUATIONS MAKE MY ADHD STRENGTHS SHINE?

Complete the sentences to learn more about which situations invite your ADHD strengths out.

My ADHD characteristics come in handy when ...

I feel grateful about the way my brain works when ...

I get on a roll and feel like I'm really making progress when ...

I think my strengths related to ADHD are ...

My brain seems to come alive when ...

I can lose track of time when I am ...

I am fascinated and curious about ...

I love learning about ...

My sweet spot is ...

Other people always admire that I can ...

I feel flooded with motivation when ...

EXPLORING MY CREATIVITY, ADHD-STYLE

People who don't have ADHD tend to think more linearly. "If I do A, then B will result." When you have more of a non-linear, ADHD-style brain, it can be a lot harder to trace a logical process for completing something. On the other hand, you might be able to think outside the box more easily and come up with different and more "out there" ideas!

To learn about your own creative process, answer these questions:

When do my most helpful ideas come to me?
(for example, on a run, while driving, in the middle of the night)

Do I have a way of tracking ideas as they come? If not, why not?

What is the easiest way for me to express a creative idea?
(for example, write it down, draw a diagram, use a whiteboard or big piece of paper)

What are some of my favorite ideas I've ever come up?

What's my favorite part of the brainstorming process?

When do I feel most alive with creativity?

Is there a time when creativity saved the day for me?

WHAT HAVE YOU LEARNED IN THIS CHAPTER?

WHAT DO YOU NOW KNOW ABOUT YOUR BRAIN AND ADHD?

CHAPTER 4

YOUR HEALTH AND ADHD

We believe it's important to examine your ADHD diagnosis across all domains of your health: physical, social, emotional and academic/occupational. This ensures you are viewing ADHD holistically, and not neglecting areas affected by your symptoms that you hadn't considered.

This is a really personal journey — it's not about measuring your health against some "gold standard." Think of it as an opportunity to look at your overall health and balance: where you feel good about your practices and where you'd like to make changes.

There's good news and there's overwhelming news. Many clients experience relief after going through this process, when they realize how broadly ADHD impacts their life. On the other hand, it can feel all-encompassing. Remember that as you treat ADHD in one aspect, it will affect other areas, which can lead to a domino effect of change.

Let's go through each area of your well-being through a critical ADHD lens.

PHYSICAL

When it comes to physical health, ADHD symptoms can get in the way of maintaining a consistent routine or being organized enough to stay on track with goals. For those who struggle with impulsivity, this can be further complicated. Traits such as poor time management can impact exercise, eating or sleep and can make finding balance feel impossible. Maybe when you work out, you overdo it, or perhaps "blockers" stop you from getting to the gym or out for a run. You may have trouble falling asleep or getting organized to go to sleep at a reasonable time, or you may become hyper-focused on another activity that delays you going to sleep.

This process is an opportunity to ask yourself, "Are ADHD symptoms getting in the way of my physical health? What is my ideal vision for improving my well-being in each area? And how important is it to me?"

SLEEP

For many individuals with ADHD, sleep can be really challenging. Some clients describe being unable to get to sleep because they have racing thoughts or are plagued by frustrations about their day. Others feel like their brain finally kicks into gear at night and they want to make use of that time.

If you think about how your executive functions should help you manage your day as well as settle your brain, it makes sense that over 50% of people with ADHD struggle with sleep hygiene in one way or another. Sorting out your experience with sleep and ADHD can be an important backbone to your overall health.

TIM: I used to think I needed three glasses of wine to settle myself enough to get to sleep. Sometimes I'd even take a Gravol. It didn't seem like a big deal. It was just a way to help myself sleep. I'd wake up at 5:00 a.m. though, with my thoughts racing again, get back to my computer and focus on work. Going through the treatment process, I saw just how numb I'd become. I started to explore what the real root of my sleep issues was all about instead of masking it.

AMY: I would get the kids (and usually my husband too) to bed and then look around and feel like this was *my* time. Some nights, I'd stay up till 2:00 or 3:00. I liked the quiet. Sometimes I'd get work done around the house, make lunches and send thank you cards. Other times ... I'm really not sure where the time went. I was sacrificing my own well-being to try to feel like my day wasn't a lost cause and do the stuff I thought I should be doing as a mom. It only made things worse. I got more and more tired, disconnected and lost.

Questions	Priority *(circle one)*	My symptoms of ADHD that affect this area are ...
Do I have difficulty falling asleep at night? Staying asleep?	*1 - none* *2 - moderate* *3 - high*	
Do I have restless thoughts at night?	*1 - none* *2 - moderate* *3 - high*	
Do I sometimes lose track of time or put off going to sleep?	*1 - none* *2 - moderate* *3 - high*	
Do I have difficulty getting up and going in the morning?	*1 - none* *2 - moderate* *3 - high*	

Tip from Coach Laura: *We see many clients struggle with putting value on sleep. Unable to put self-care high on their list, they often compensate for other inefficiencies by not prioritizing sleep. This can create a cycle where their symptoms are exacerbated by lack of sleep. That cycle can be difficult to break. Value your own well-being by getting regular sleep — it can have a dramatic effect. You deserve sleep and you need it!*

NUTRITION

When you have untreated ADHD, healthy eating habits can be elusive. Perhaps it's hard to find the time to be organized about food, to have the groceries around and to make something. Or maybe symptoms of impulsivity get in the way, with a tendency to binge or eat what you feel like in the moment. Or you might forget to eat for hours, and then find yourself with few options when you finally come up for air. ADHD symptoms can interfere with sustainable healthy eating practices and even create secondary symptoms such as headaches, lethargy, lightheadedness or irritability.

JASON: I've always eaten my feelings. The way I felt about myself affected what I consumed — I just hadn't made the connection. I guess somewhere inside me, I knew that bingeing was a way for me to let go, to give in to all my out-of-control feelings, but it wasn't until I understood ADHD that I connected all the dots. Eating was this place where I could stop trying to keep myself in line and give in to the impulsivity. I mean, I always knew I had eating issues, but I didn't know why I had them. Once I saw how my ADHD fueled them, I was able to figure out how to make changes.

CANDACE: From as young as I can remember, food felt like work. My parents were always trying to get me to finish my dinner, but I would be daydreaming or wanting to go do something else. I think I had too much going on in my head to enjoy eating. Food was this nuisance that got in the way of my other interests. I ate like a bird and hated when my foods touched each other — maybe I was trying to keep it organized because it was one thing I could control. My food palate was basic and weird and held me back in social situations.

When I realized I had ADHD, I started to pull apart my relationship with eating and began the journey to being more normal with food. Now I'm working on seeing how it can be enjoyable and figuring out how to let myself be more adventurous. I'm making progress, but I still don't think I'll ever like sushi!

Questions	Priority (circle one)	My symptoms of ADHD that affect this area are ...
Do I eat healthy and consistent meals?	1 - none 2 - moderate 3 - high	
Am I an impulsive eater?	1 - none 2 - moderate 3 - high	
Do I sometimes forget to eat?	1 - none 2 - moderate 3 - high	
Do I enjoy food?	1 - none 2 - moderate 3 - high	
Do I have difficulty organizing meals or grocery shopping?	1 - none 2 - moderate 3 - high	

Tip from Coach Laura: *Building healthy nutritional habits is a complicated behavior change goal. It might sound easy to start packing a healthy lunch or not eat after 8:00 pm., but many clients have to do significant work to understand what's getting in the way of their nutritional goals.*

Not only does healthy eating require planning and structure (two things that are often difficult if you have ADHD), but in many cases, there's emotional work to do as well. Before jumping to the goal-setting process, figure out the root of your challenges.

PHYSICAL ACTIVITY

ADHD symptoms can get in the way of regular exercise. Maybe it's because your goals are too big ("It's not worth working out unless I have a whole hour of free time"), or perhaps you are too behind on other things to feel like you can make exercise a priority. Maybe you don't remember how to have fun in exercise anymore, or you feel like you can barely get through your day, so how could you possibly fit in one more thing?

Fitting in exercise does require significant planning and likely some creative thinking. In fact, getting regular exercise is a challenge for everyone, even those without ADHD. But research shows that exercise can give you a neurotransmitter boost (think dopamine and serotonin levels), which can also help engage the prefrontal cortex and executive functions. It's like a natural medication. Understanding the importance of this might encourage you to add regular physical activity to your life.

TIM: I had no physical activity or any outlet in my life for over a decade. I guess I'd stopped thinking it was important and didn't even know where to start. I was tense all the time, plagued by my own stress, and had gained weight. I didn't know how to play with my kids, and the thought of showing up at a gym had no appeal to me.

When I started walking 20 minutes a day, I had relief from my stress during this pocket of time. I listened to music again, which I really enjoyed. I think that's when I began to forgive myself slowly — a subtle shift that felt like a huge difference in my life.

AMY: I was doing everything for everyone and nothing for myself. I'm not saying that in some "I am so generous" way, it's just what I thought I *should* be doing. Time for me was the lowest of my priorities, and doing a workout class felt completely out of the question. I was a personal trainer who never worked out. It seems so crazy to say that now.

I started meeting a friend at the gym. First it was once a week and eventually we made it up to three times. It's changed my life. I get to have friend time, and I feel so much more able to access calm in my mind. Looking back, I can't believe I wasn't doing this. It's my way of finding some fun in my life, and it's reminded me that I am worth something, too. I'm even hoping to get back into seeing clients again soon.

Questions	Priority *(circle one)*	My symptoms of ADHD that affect this area are ...
Do I exercise consistently?	1 - none 2 - moderate 3 - high	
Do I participate in any formal exercise?	1 - none 2 - moderate 3 - high	
Do I use exercise strategically (in other words, to help focus)?	1 - none 2 - moderate 3 - high	

Tip from Dr. Anne: *We know it can be hard to stay on track with goals and maintain routines when you have ADHD. It helps if you can structure physical activity into your regular environment, like going for a walk at lunchtime, taking the stairs, using a fitness app on your phone (even 20 minutes a day) or meeting a friend on the way home for a walk or run (instead of a drink!). With regular exercise, you'll feel better and be armed to make smarter, more efficient choices. It's not only beneficial for addressing symptoms of ADHD, it's also a great mood and anxiety management practice.*

SUBSTANCE USE

Untreated ADHD can put you at risk for substance use issues, sometimes viewed as self-medicating. Some individuals describe it as a way to dull their feelings of restlessness or calm their mind. Others use it as a way to fall asleep or feel more excitement in their lives.

An indicator of a substance issue being linked to ADHD is when it feels like a coping mechanism, rather than a fun social activity. Others with significant impulsivity-control challenges struggle with knowing their limit and have difficulty with moderation. Understanding your relationship with substances and assessing whether it is linked to ADHD symptoms can be a powerful and illuminating experience.

JASON: I drank a lot when I was at school, but then again, so did everyone. It's not like I was drinking every day, but when I started, I knew I wasn't going to stop until I got blackout drunk. It brought out my fun self — the life-of-the-party self — which was how everyone liked to see me. Jovial, funny, really out there. For a few hours, I'd feel better, forget all my stresses. But I'd wake up feeling terrible about myself. The work I had to do was still there, but the crushing guilt made it hard to get going at all.

When I started to heal, I had to learn that, just because it was fun for those around me, that person wasn't my best self. I realized I didn't like being the class clown. That was me overcompensating for the way I actually felt — small, out of control and insecure. I had to learn to look in the mirror and say, "Hey, Jason, where are you at?" Then I could make choices that were right for me.

TIM: As I more honestly asked myself why I was drinking, I saw how it was connected to my feelings about myself and my symptoms of ADHD. It was a way for me to avoid seeing the truth: I had no idea what I was doing day-to-day and just kept stepping back on the treadmill. When I finally needed to unwind and get some sleep, I turned to wine as a way to help settle all my inner turmoil. Now that I see this, I'm getting to a place where I can imagine falling asleep naturally.

Tip from Dr. Anne: ADHD and substance use issues can be related, and some individuals struggle with substance use to the point where support and treatment for addiction is recommended. In these cases, treating addictions issues takes priority over getting support for symptoms of ADHD, as the impairment and impact on functioning can be significant. If you have concerns in this area, discuss with your medical practitioner or reach out to a mental health counselor.

Questions	Priority (circle one)	My symptoms of ADHD that affect this area are ...
Do I smoke/drink/use any other drugs? If so, how often and when?	*1 - none* *2 - moderate* *3 - high*	
Do I consider substance use a concern?	*1 - none* *2 - moderate* *3 - high*	
How much caffeine do I consume on average? How does it make me feel?	*1 - none* *2 - moderate* *3 - high*	

Tip from Coach Laura: *Understanding the effect a substance has on your brain and your well-being can help you determine whether it's a healthy use or a hindrance to your goals. For example, nicotine and caffeine are stimulants that can temporarily support ADHD by enhancing access to your prefrontal cortex and executive functions. (We, of course, don't recommend smoking but want to help you understand the effect you may receive from smoking.)*

Alcohol, on the other hand, can be a depressant and may help you relax temporarily. Usually, it allows individuals to mask feelings for a period of time. However, post-drinking, feelings of anxiety or frustration may return with even more fervor. Some people report they are even worse and exhibit periods of low mood. Taking an objective view of substance use and how it is part of your life can help you get to the root of where you want to go and the choices you want to make.

SCREEN USE

The internet was basically designed for people with ADHD — there's always something interesting and stimulating at your fingertips. But internet-connected devices and screens can make ADHD symptoms even more challenging to control. Many of our clients feel they get stuck in a "time warp" when they start on the internet. This technology has also made it harder to separate home from work.

Screen use can get in the way of sleep, productivity, safe driving and being present with your family and make work that requires full concentration even more difficult to engage in. Certainly technology can be helpful, but this requires conscious limitations and structure.

JASON: I'd watch series after series on Netflix when I couldn't bear to face my schoolwork or the reality of how I was feeling. I'd go to the library, put headphones on and pretend to study. My housemates would be cramming, but the thought of opening a book made me so anxious, I'd just tune out instead. I don't even want to share how many hours a day I spent mindlessly watching. When football season ended, that's when things really fell apart and I retreated. Now that I'm on the other side of this, I can't believe how dark those days were.

AMY: For a few years, I was totally obsessed with my phone — it was always with me. I was texting everyone, not realizing how much time I was spending on it. I was a personal trainer who was saying I didn't have time for exercise, but when I became more mindful about it, I discovered I was spending over three hours a day messaging and using social media.

This was a key insight because when I wanted more physical activity and meditation in my life, reducing my screen usage was an easy way to regain time. By reducing the distractions of social media, I was able to quickly shift my priorities and improve my time management. Not to mention that social media often made me feel bad about myself and wasn't a good motivator, at least the way I was using it.

Questions	Priority *(circle one)*	My symptoms of ADHD that affect this area are ...
Do I spend too much time on screens such as TV, computers and video games?	1 - none 2 - moderate 3 - high	
Does my screen use get in the way of other activities (for example, sleep, chores, spending time with others)?	1 - none 2 - moderate 3 - high	
Do I have strategies to control my screen use?	1 - none 2 - moderate 3 - high	

Tip from Dr. Anne: *Given what we know about the brain, it makes sense that so many people with ADHD struggle to achieve balance with screen use. The ADHD brain is wired to want highly stimulating, fast-paced information. When people with ADHD are being entertained, in an engaging experience, they can feel a kind of euphoria. It can then be difficult to transition focus to something more mundane, like reviewing a document or studying for an exam.*

Being aware of your screen use, and sorting out if it's getting in the way of your priorities, is helpful. In our experience, there's good news in this area. Often when you know what you want your screen use to look like, it's an easy area to change parameters in. Ironically, there are lots of great apps that help control use, too.

SOCIAL

ADHD's impact in the area of social well-being is often trickier to identify than in more obvious domains, like school or work. Symptoms can get miscategorized as personal characteristics or traits, so the individual and those around them mistake executive functioning issues as overt personality flaws. For example, impulsivity can give an impression of harshness, or inattention can get in the way of making social connections or contributing well as a team member. This is not to say these symptoms should be accepted or are appropriate, but by connecting them with a brain difference, you can better understand how to make changes, as opposed to throwing up your hands and saying "That's just me."

For some individuals with ADHD, the opposite situation may be the case. Their strengths or gifts are in connecting with others and they hyper-focus on helping others. In these cases, they are often driven by what they think others want them to do. Sometimes, they self-identify as "pleasers." This can look okay from the outside, but can have negative outcomes, including a loss of self-awareness and challenges setting personal limitations and, ultimately, managing priorities and making decisions. A diagnosis of ADHD can help you see where your symptoms may be affecting your social life and help you sort out where to go from there.

HOME LIFE ROUTINES

Nowadays our households are busier than ever. We all need our executive functions to manage everything from getting out the door on time to limiting distractions to keeping our home lives organized and balanced. This lifestyle is complicated, and competing interests for our time make it hard to maintain a feeling of control in our home life.

Individuals with ADHD often feel like they don't want routines and push back on things that seem too monotonous. Perhaps it comes from a fear of not being able to stick to commitments or a concern that too much structure will be boring. Keep in mind that structure often reduces stress and helps you stay on top of habits that will make you feel more in control.

CANDACE: My routines had gotten out of hand. I needed everything just so and never invited anyone over. In an effort to keep myself organized and on top of things, I'd labeled pretty much everything in my apartment. I would eat the same boring meals on a rotation and did absolutely nothing sporadic.

When I figured out what I needed to change in my home life, the biggest change was learning to actually leave my home. It started with a 20-minute walk each morning. From there, I began the slow process of conquering one thing after another.

AMY: I had to learn to "let go." Two simple words, but when you're someone who has definitely not been letting things go her whole life, it was really hard to do. But letting go helped me stop running circles around the house. For a while, things got messier, which was stressful, but that needed to happen so I could have a chance at peace in a home with three kids.

Once I saw my home routine more objectively, I noticed a lot that could be done more strategically. We got a professional organizer to come to the house and help set us up for success, including having our children help with chores. This made a difference, too. Mentally and physically, I had to stop carrying it all invisibly around my neck.

Questions	Priority (circle one)	My symptoms of ADHD that affect this area are ...
Do I have any consistency in my life?	*1 - none* *2 - moderate* *3 - high*	
Do I have bedtime and morning routines?	*1 - none* *2 - moderate* *3 - high*	
Do I wish I had more routines at home? If so, during which part of my day?	*1 - none* *2 - moderate* *3 - high*	

Tip from Coach Laura: *Sometimes a few tweaks in your home life routine make a difference in your day-to-day. It may be having more healthy prepared groceries in the fridge, introducing a sleep routine or scheduling time for play with your children or partner. Be careful about setting goals that are too lofty or introduce too big of a change. A few subtle tweaks might be enough and will be easier to maintain.*

MONEY MANAGEMENT

ADHD can get in the way of sustainable money management. Sometimes impulsive spending is the problem. In other cases, individuals describe a lack of ability to organize or focus long enough to stay on track with any long-term financial planning, so they end up not being connected or consistent with a budget or financial plan. Couples affected by ADHD may find this an area of high conflict. It is difficult for many people to stay on top of financial planning — ADHD symptoms can make it all the more challenging.

JASON: You can imagine what my ability to manage money was like before this whole process started. Between my impulsive eating and drinking and serious lack of long-term thinking, I was emailing my parents every month asking for more money. I had overdue books at the library and had missed tuition payments. I spent my money for books on everything but books. My money management was just another indicator of the ups and downs of my life.

I still struggle with it. It's so hard for me to stay engaged and consistent. At least I don't freak out on my parents when we talk about it now (that's an improvement), and I really am trying to take responsibility. We've agreed on a weekly allowance, so that I focus on one week at a time. That's helped, but we're still figuring it out.

TIM: Me and money. Talk about an unhealthy relationship — add it to the list! I was obsessed with money, pretty good at tracking it and never felt like I had enough. I was so focused on making more and more. It wasn't that I was bad at money management per se — it was sort of an area of hyper-focus, but to a negative extent.

I'd be so illogical about it, too. Jane would buy our kids new shoes and I'd be in a bad mood about it, but then I'd buy us a bigger house and spend on other luxuries I thought would make us happy (or show success). I don't know. It wasn't rational, and we're lucky I was able to put away a lot, because now I really want to enjoy life.

Questions	Priority *(circle one)*	My symptoms of ADHD that affect this area are ...
Do I spend impulsively?	1 - none 2 - moderate 3 - high	
Is it difficult to keep track of my spending or bills?	1 - none 2 - moderate 3 - high	
Do I have a system in place for keeping track of my budget? If not, why not?	1 - none 2 - moderate 3 - high	

Tip from Dr. Anne: *Many Springboard clients have put financial planning as a low priority — at first — but over time realized it's a bigger priority. While it may not be at the forefront of concerns, money management is such a backbone for making lifestyle choices and feeling a sense of accomplishment and control.*

If more proactive financial planning would make a difference in your ability to follow through on your well-being goals, we recommend that you work with a professional (administrative assistant, financial planner, accountant) to get on track.

DRIVING AWARENESS

Driving is a great example of the prefrontal cortex at work. While you're keeping your eyes on what lies ahead, you're constantly assessing cars around you, making decisions in the moment and managing multiple conflicting pieces of information at the same time. Now add symptoms like inattention, hyper-focusing, impulsivity and general time management concerns to the mix, and driving (and parking) can become a significant problem for people with ADHD. Interestingly, some people find they're able to engage while driving because it can be so stimulating, and they don't report the same challenges.

TIM: I've always felt that I'm a great driver. I drive fast but have never been in an accident. When I drive, I feel like I almost hyper-focus. Even if I'm running late or need to get somewhere fast, I get into a zone. When I started learning about ADHD though — and once I was more honest with myself — I had to admit that, even though I could react quickly, I was taking too many risks.

I used to get defensive when Jane would say she didn't want to drive with me or worried when the kids were with me in the car. I'd get so angry at her. But now I understand where she's coming from, and I guess now I honestly care how she feels in the car. All part of the process. But I *am* an excellent driver — just want to be clear about that!

AMY: Oh wow, I've been lucky too many times with driving. I'm so grateful nothing has happened while I was texting, or reaching for something, or putting on makeup on the go. I've even caught myself zoning out and have had to pull myself back: "Amy, you're driving right now. Get yourself together." It's not that I'm a crazy speeder or road-rager or anything, but if I had to count the number of times I've put myself or my kids in danger by losing focus ... sheesh. I don't like to think about it.

Coming to terms with this through my ADHD diagnosis was maybe one of the single most important realizations from a safety perspective. I take my time behind the wheel a lot more seriously now. My phone is in the back out of reach, I don't let myself do other things at the same time, and I even try to remember where I'm going!

Questions	Priority (circle one)	My symptoms of ADHD that affect this area are ...
Am I aggressive, impulsive or impatient while driving?	1 - none 2 - moderate 3 - high	
Have I had any accidents or tickets?	1 - none 2 - moderate 3 - high	
Do I often have to drive more aggressively because of time management concerns?	1 - none 2 - moderate 3 - high	

Tip from Coach Laura: *Many of our clients have challenges or difficulties when it comes to driving awareness, but each story is different. Some struggle with speeding or parking tickets or emotional regulation while driving. Others share that they've never gotten their driver's license because they didn't think it was a good idea.*

ADHD symptoms can impact driving in many ways. Coming to terms with whether symptoms affect your driving can help you avoid dangerous situations. To get an objective take on your driving skills, ask a family member how they experience your driving. Often, our clients initially claim driving isn't an issue, but later admit they're lucky nothing has ever happened.

COMMUNICATION

ADHD can impact your ability to communicate, and symptoms can often alter how you're perceived. For example, individuals with symptoms of impulsivity can have an almost overbearing presence. They often think fast, talk fast and can't wait for those around them to finish their thought before an answer or another question comes out. Sometimes they're fearful of forgetting their idea and struggle to stop themselves and let others finish their thoughts.

Clients with symptoms of inattention describe a different experience, one where they struggle to get their words out in a clear way. Often held back by anxiety or difficulties pulling their thoughts together, they tend to under-participate in groups.

To improve communication in your personal and professional environments, assess whether symptoms affect how you tend to communicate.

JASON: Actually I think communication is one of my strengths, sort of a gift that has come with my ADHD symptoms. I've always been kind and big-hearted, and I'm good at boosting others up. I also have a way with words, which is probably how I got so far without being diagnosed — I could talk my way out of anything. I can show up late, pull off a last-minute presentation and still make a good impression.

Since being diagnosed, though, I've been working at listening and communicating more authentically. I try to really take in what others have to say, and when I'm talking, I make sure it's not just what people want to hear from me, but what makes me feel whole.

AMY: I've always been quiet, timid and shy. For as long as I can remember, I've clammed up in situations where I need to speak on the spot. In grade school, I would tremble at the thought of being called on in class. I just couldn't get my thoughts out in an organized way. I've never been comfortable participating in social settings, even small ones. I get so easily distracted and feel like I can never keep up. By the time I decide I want to share something, the conversation has moved on.

Since beginning the treatment process, I've been able to see more clearly that I'm missing out in these situations. Before, I don't think I realized it. This awareness has helped me take small steps to participating more and seeing that my voice matters, too. It hasn't been easy, but I'm getting there.

Questions	Priority (circle one)	My symptoms of ADHD that affect this area are ...
Do I feel as though I talk too much — or not enough?	1 - none 2 - moderate 3 - high	
Do I have difficulty articulating myself?	1 - none 2 - moderate 3 - high	
Do I tend to interrupt or speak at inappropriate times?	1 - none 2 - moderate 3 - high	
Am I a word wizard who can smooth-talk my way out of anything?	1 - none 2 - moderate 3 - high	
Do I express my feelings or opinions to others?	1 - none 2 - moderate 3 - high	

Tip from Dr. Anne: *To better understand how people see your communication style, ask someone you trust how you come across. You may not realize your impact on others, and your intentions of how you want to come across might not match up with your actions. Try not to be defensive. This is about gaining data so your true self can be heard more clearly.*

RELATIONSHIPS

Once you identify your individual symptoms of ADHD, you quickly see how they affect your relationships. Especially if you aren't diagnosed until adulthood, the process can feel overwhelming to work through. Suddenly, there's an opportunity to reconcile both past and present relationships with this newly identified elephant in the room.

Sometimes ADHD symptoms hold you back from something more logistical, like texting or emailing friends. In other cases, the implications might be deeper, such as building or maintaining intimacy with the people you care about.

TIM: Well, let's put it this way: when I finally admitted to myself I had ADHD, I pretty much had no one left. I'd gone through the diagnosis process (quite reluctantly), and at some point, things started to make sense and I looked at everything through a new lens.

I'd lost so many relationships and was detached from those who'd stuck around. I'd never gotten that close to people, always guarded, but I'd been so bad at maintaining contact with friends and family, that by a certain point I wasn't seeing anyone socially at all. I was a million miles away in almost every social setting I found myself in, even at home.

This was the single most important area of well-being for me to sort out. I honestly feel like a different person. I'm getting more present at home, have connected with old friends and have even been making new ones!

AMY: I don't know exactly when the fallout happened. Probably after I got married. I was more anxious, feeling like I couldn't keep up. I cut out social time and distanced myself from friends and even family. I guess I wanted to be an attentive wife and mother or something? I just knew I had to cut things out if I was going to manage a household.

In some ways, focusing on the kids has been great, but it's also taken me away from being aware of my own needs. And of course, it's a spiral. So my healing process has been a lot about rebuilding relationships. Thankfully! I can't believe how I pushed away so many people who were close to me.

Questions	Priority (circle one)	My symptoms of ADHD that affect this area are ...
Are the relationships in my life positive?	1 - none 2 - moderate 3 - high	
Do I spend enough time with others?	1 - none 2 - moderate 3 - high	
Do I have a tough time keeping in touch with people?	1 - none 2 - moderate 3 - high	
Do I have difficulty keeping commitments?	1 - none 2 - moderate 3 - high	

Tip from Dr. Anne: *It's always one of the hardest realizations for our clients when they see how ADHD symptoms have hurt both past and present relationships. That understanding often comes with some really tough feelings. It can be discouraging when you think you don't have many people left in your life.*

That being said, you can make changes in this area even now. Reaching out to friends and family with a clearer awareness of yourself often brings people closer quite quickly. We frequently see our clients authentically re-engage with their communities once they can overcome the "blockers" that have been holding them back. So, don't be afraid to reach out to relationships from the past with your newfound understanding of your symptoms. It is likely worth the tough first phone call!

PHYSICAL INTIMACY/SEX

Connected physical intimacy requires you to be in the moment and willing to openly share oneself. Undiagnosed ADHD can be a barrier to intimate relations in a number of ways. Logistically, difficulties with time management can hinder you from making the time and space to share with your partner. Mentally, symptoms of distractibility and restlessness can contribute to feelings of distance. Symptoms of impulsivity can be a risk factor for making unsafe or ill-conceived sexual decisions. Finally, secondary symptoms such as anxiety, depression, low self-esteem and high conflict in relationships can directly or indirectly impact this area.

TIM: For me, this was a high priority from the beginning. Honestly, I felt kind of ripped off. Jane never wanted to have sex and spent most of the time criticizing everything I did. At least, that's how I saw it. I was defensive, hurt and angry about the way she was treating me. It took a long time to shed those feelings of blame and "woe is me." But if we were ever going to connect again, I had to leave that headspace. Eventually, thankfully, I did get out of that place, and I'm so grateful I did.

Looking back, I see things more clearly. How could she have wanted to be intimate with someone who was so emotionally unavailable? Intimacy took a long time for us rebuild. It was one of the last things for us to connect on. We're getting there now, but we're still working on it. We had to forgive, let the past be the past and start to care for each other again.

AMY: This was an area I didn't really care about, or at least thought I didn't care about. I was sort of in a state of permanent anxiety, constantly in my own head. I could never relax my brain enough to consider being intimate with my husband. He tried for a while but eventually gave up. We were like roommates — we got along pretty well but we'd lost any passion or feelings of romance.

It took a long time for me to step outside myself and realize I wanted to connect with him and that sex didn't have to be another "chore." It sounds crazy but I had to see how it could be joyful and satisfying. To do that, I had to come to terms with and treat my anxiety and distractibility. My husband was patient, and we're now in a much better place. I had to take pressure off myself, and we both had to start actually talking to each other.

Questions	Priority *(circle one)*	My symptoms of ADHD that affect this area are ...
Do I have physical or emotional difficulties being intimate with my partner?	1 - none 2 - moderate 3 - high	
Am I distractible and disengaged during sex?	1 - none 2 - moderate 3 - high	
Am I impulsive with sex or intimate relationships?	1 - none 2 - moderate 3 - high	

Tip from Coach Laura: *For many couples we've worked with, physical intimacy has been a challenging health domain to address. When a couple isn't feeling satisfied with their level of intimacy, the "roadmap" to creating sustainable change in this area can be complicated. It often requires building new trust, reconnecting on an emotional level and each partner focusing on self-work before the couple can take a positive step. Partners must be patient with each other.*

Intimacy is often one of the later steps in the healing process, once other relationship challenges have been sorted out. That being said, don't wait too long. Taking steps physically can often help build closeness and be a powerful motivator to finding happiness in your relationship.

Being intimate doesn't have to be an "all or nothing" decision either. Remember holding hands? Starting slow? These small steps toward healing, both emotional and physical, can be a powerful catalyst. Other variables — such as stress, confidence or hormonal changes — can also affect intimacy, so take time to unpack what's going on for you.

EMOTIONAL

ADHD symptoms can impact emotional awareness and regulation in several respects, especially when it comes to feeling "on or off" with emotions. People with ADHD often describe feeling either flooded with emotions or kind of disconnected. It can be hard to feel balanced in this area of well-being. Symptoms of inattention can make you unaware of your emotions, whereas symptoms of impulsivity can create an almost explosive expression of emotions.

When ADHD goes undiagnosed for a long time, there's often a major disconnect between your emotional state and your wants and needs. Finding balance and being aware of what nourishes and energizes you are crucial to achieving a more authentic emotional experience.

STRESS MANAGEMENT

Managing stress is challenging for everyone nowadays, and with undiagnosed or untreated ADHD in the picture, it's even more complicated. Stress is frequently masked by other coping strategies, or may come in waves depending on your symptoms. Individuals with ADHD are often calm during high-stress situations, as their prefrontal cortex "wakes up" in situations of danger or urgency. This may explain why many high-stress jobs are a good fit for someone with ADHD — they thrive on "putting out fires."

But daily stressors that aren't necessarily "fires" but that build over time can be tough on individuals with ADHD. When there isn't an engaging need in front of them, they can be "off" or distractible. In some cases, significant symptoms of anxiety make managing stress challenging and hold back individuals from taking risks or finding their areas of strength. Overall, many of our clients struggle with managing day-to-day life without significant support from those around them.

JASON: Stress management, eh? What's that? No, I'm kidding. It's hard to put into words my journey in this area. It's not my favorite thing to talk about, but it's important. If I'm being honest and clinical about it, I managed my stress by partying, avoiding it as much as possible and binge eating. I had to do a lot of work to come to terms with both what was stressing me out and what I was doing about it day-to-day.

I'm still working hard at this. Actually, the moments when I'm working on handling my stress are when I most wish I'd been diagnosed when I was younger. I've created so many extra challenges and secondary issues by not being honest with myself. You would have said I was super easygoing, and that's how I looked to others. But inside, I've been tied up in knots for as long as I can remember.

CANDACE: I always confused stress and anxiety, but when I started to unpack them, I realized there were work situations that could be considered high-stakes that made me feel less anxious! For example, when we had to troubleshoot for a client on a deadline, I could focus and forget my other worries. It was hard and took mental effort and energy, but it wasn't the same kind of stress or anxiety I felt about the daily stuff I wasn't getting done.

Taxes were the worst. Every year, the same intense stress would build. When I eventually got around to finding the papers and digging into it, it never seemed as bad as I'd made it out to be. I get more organized each year, so it's a little less stressful.

Questions	Priority (circle one)	My symptoms of ADHD that affect this area are ...
Do I easily get overwhelmed?	1 - none 2 - moderate 3 - high	
Do I connect with stress, or do I disengage from it?	1 - none 2 - moderate 3 - high	
Do I internalize or externalize stress?	1 - none 2 - moderate 3 - high	
Do I have strategies in place to deal with stress?	1 - none 2 - moderate 3 - high	

Tip from Coach Laura: *Becoming aware of your stress triggers and their roots, and exploring how you want your day-to-day to look, can be empowering. Our clients are often able to quickly make significant changes in this area once they name what stresses them out and strategize changes in their everyday life to reach specific goals.*

Something small, like having a place for your keys, is an example of an easy change that significantly impacts your headspace as you try to leave for work on time every morning. By putting value on where you leave your keys when you get home, you can start your day more calmly. It's a small change with a big reward, which can then have knock-on effects throughout the day to build positive momentum.

ANGER MANAGEMENT

ADHD symptoms can seriously get in the way of managing anger. Individuals with symptoms of impulsivity can be easily frustrated and explosive, describing "big feelings" or "flooding." They're often quick to get over their reactions as well. Their anger might come in a burst, then quickly dissipate.

Individuals with predominantly inattentive symptoms describe almost an opposite effect, where they over-apologize and don't allow themselves to feel angry. They tend to carry these feelings, which often results in them being hard on themselves, whether they realize it or not.

Anger is a healthy, vital emotion, and exploring this area of well-being is important in sorting out your self-identity and fostering a more balanced self-view.

CANDACE: I'm the "quiet as a mouse" type of ADHD. I've literally never shown anger my whole life. When I went through diagnosis and treatment, this area felt unimportant at first. It's not like I was ever actually angry, so I thought I was managing anger well.

But when I understood more about my feelings, I saw I was taking anger and frustration out on myself a lot. I was also avoiding so many situations in order to never risk putting my feelings on the line.

I don't think you'll ever see me angry in the hot sense of the word, but I'm learning to put myself out there more, and I've stopped apologizing for everything. I'm getting there.

TIM: I'm always saying to Jane now, "Thanks for putting up with all that." I was a ball of anger. If things weren't going the way I wanted, I was quick to blame others. I was defensive, aggressive and unaware of how I came across. I could go from zero to a hundred so fast. Weirdly though, in other instances, I could also disengage quickly — like weirdly fast. I could be so mad about something and then basically forget about it five minutes later.

Now, analyzing more clearly, I guess I'd lose focus and then be over it. Jane would be trying to put the pieces together and I'd have moved on. It's hard to explain. It feels backward or illogical. What's really strange is that at work, I was known for my cool demeanor in high-pressure or frustrating situations. I never flared up like I did at home.

Questions	Priority (circle one)	My symptoms of ADHD that affect this area are ...
Do I express anger or frustration outwardly or do I keep it inside?	1 - none 2 - moderate 3 - high	
Do I react impulsively when feeling angry or frustrated?	1 - none 2 - moderate 3 - high	
Do I get angry at myself?	1 - none 2 - moderate 3 - high	

Tip from Coach Laura: *Remember "getting upset about being upset"? Many undiagnosed individuals hold in their anger toward others and instead take it out on themselves. You might not think of this as an anger management issue, but if you find yourself saying something like "I never get angry," you might want to explore whether you internalize feelings and end up damaging your own headspace, even though you don't get visibly mad at others. This behavior may be related to a self-narrative you've experienced for a long time.*

Let's imagine you feel angry or frustrated with your partner because of how they're treating you. Maybe they're speaking in a way that feels belittling. Instead of expressing how you feel, you apologize, because you think it's easier that way, or because you aren't good at communicating in the moment. You end up agreeing to your partner's terms, instead of standing up for yourself.

Even if it reduces conflict in the short term, this acquiescence might be damaging your ability to connect with people around you. Anger (in moderation) is an important and healthy part of being human. Learning how to constructively express your anger, instead of internalizing or "bottling it up," is an important part of managing your emotions sustainably.

HEALTHY OUTLET EXPRESSION

When ADHD goes undiagnosed or untreated for a long time, individuals often give up on things they love to do. Sometimes it's because it's such an effort to manage other responsibilities and priorities, and often it is related to struggles with organization and time management. But by walking away from things that are fun or stimulating for your brain, you can end up losing motivation for other things. Our clients describe being in a "twilight zone," where they feel numb.

Individuals diagnosed with ADHD frequently set goals of finding calm, joy and balance. Rediscovering something you used to love doing can be an impactful part of treatment.

JASON: Healthy outlets appeared as opposed to all the unhealthy outlets I had. Like I said earlier, I started with one healthy outlet: walking my dog. I found it peaceful and chill to throw her sticks and watch her come running back. Being outside, and this simple act — for the first time in a long time, I could breathe. Football, I loved and missed, and I knew I needed sport back in my life. But I also knew that competitive sport brought pressure and feelings I didn't want to get back to.

First I wanted to add things that were more personal. So I started with simple hangouts with friends and volunteering with kids, and then I joined an adult running group. I was the youngest, and at first, I didn't feel very comfortable. But, actually, it was amazing. I met great mentors and found that it helped me reduce stress, gain perspective from others in the group and find some stability and balance. It was also really nice to do something active with zero pressure on my performance.

AMY: Joy and fun were two words I didn't identify with for a few decades. I wasn't depressed in bed like you might be picturing. I was just spinning from thing to thing. I was everywhere and nowhere. Once I started working out, things definitely got better. Meditation really helped too.

Another fun thing that came back into my life was music. I'd always loved music. For much of my life, it was an outlet for me and then I forgot about it. I didn't know how to put music on my phone and so lived without. For my birthday this year, I asked for a speaker system, and my husband and kids set it up with my phone and added playlists that I love. My kids noticed immediately how my mood lifted. We started having family dance parties, and I could cook dinner with a better headspace. It made an unexpectedly big difference for me.

Questions	Priority (circle one)	My symptoms of ADHD that affect this area are ...
Do I have ways to relieve stress or negative feelings?	1 - none 2 - moderate 3 - high	
Do I express my feelings to others or have an outlet to express feelings (for example, writing)?	1 - none 2 - moderate 3 - high	
Do I participate in things that make me feel good or proud?	1 - none 2 - moderate 3 - high	
Do I have activities in my life that I enjoy? If so, how often? If not, why not?	1 - none 2 - moderate 3 - high	

Tip from Dr. Anne: *Joy and passion are two of the great motivators. We regularly hear from our clients that they don't have anything "fun" going on in their lives, but they used to have a lot of interests. They've just pulled back on them because they couldn't keep up. We often spend significant time exploring the layers of these decisions.*

At Springboard, we believe in solution-focused and strengths-based behavior goals and the importance of programming in "joy" as one of your goals. Ensuring your goals and action plans include things you find pleasurable is key to creating sustainable behavior change and enjoying life.

CONNECTING WITH OTHERS

When it comes to ADHD, connecting with others can be a huge strength. Naturally passionate about people, many individuals with ADHD share themselves easily and in the moment. For others, this is a difficult area, especially if they don't have a clear understanding of who they are separate from their symptoms or who they can be. It may be hard to gather your thoughts and figure out how to articulate yourself in a way that makes you feel good. Overall, it can be challenging to maintain healthy, connected relationships when mental health symptoms override kind and caring intentions. In addition, maintaining connections requires organization and time management strategies now more than ever.

CANDACE: I've always been painfully shy and — now I know — also experience symptoms of anxiety, especially in social situations. Between my ADHD symptoms and my anxiety, I seem to avoid almost every type of social interaction that approaches connection. I've never had a real boyfriend, and I can count the number of close friends I've had on one hand. I'm close to those I know really well, though. I tend to be kind to a fault, and I think people appreciate my genuine interest in them. But if I'm being honest, I still have lots of work to do in this area. I know where I want to go, but I'm taking baby steps.

TIM: I've been able to make good friends and read people well in certain aspects of my life, but I've always been hesitant to let people in to know me. Even in the diagnosis process, when we talked about my ability to connect with others, I wasn't sure what to say. I feel like it's been kind of okay most of my life, like I've always been able to make friends and stuff. Still, when things get hard for me, social connections are one of the first things I pull away from. Most importantly, I see now that I'd pulled away from the people I cared about most — my wife and kids.

I'm far from a social misfit, but I don't have this figured out yet either. I'm still working on how to prioritize connecting with others — that includes continuing to learn how to share myself, too. These are my major priorities.

Questions	Priority (circle one)	My symptoms of ADHD that affect this area are ...
Do I connect well with a lot of people but not on a deeper level?	1 - none 2 - moderate 3 - high	
Am I a pleaser?	1 - none 2 - moderate 3 - high	
Do I have difficulty connecting with others or can I read people well?	1 - none 2 - moderate 3 - high	

Tip from Coach Laura: *Watch for when a strength might actually be getting in the way of self-care. We definitely have gotten to know clients who are really well liked and keenly generous about helping others. For example, they might be offering their time with work or advice and then get to the end of their work day and have neglected to do their own priorities. These traits can be well-intentioned, but they can still be a barrier to achieving balance and connection, especially for those closest to the individual. Put simply, make sure you are not being distracted by helping others.*

SELF-ESTEEM MAINTENANCE

The symptoms associated with ADHD get in the way of building self-awareness and, ultimately, positive and sustainable self-esteem. For children with ADHD, the symptoms can often look willful and be damaging to building confidence in their abilities. Sometimes they create habits that are hurtful to themselves and others. These feelings and this history can carry over into adulthood and be even more detrimental, catalyzing secondary symptoms and a long list of disappointments.

A huge benefit of identifying a diagnosis of ADHD is that it allows you to come to terms with a new self-identity. This "naming" can help you create new awareness, leading to more sustainable goals and realistic expectations.

JASON: I think I'm pretty classic in this area. Hugely confident on the outside, trying to live up to everyone's expectations of me, but inside feeling like a failure. I was hiding from my work and the responsibilities I couldn't get done. Joking around about it and brushing it off didn't help. "I'll study later, right?" But deep down, I was feeling out of control with my eating and drinking and basically feeling terrible about myself.

For me, this diagnosis was about admitting I wasn't okay and hadn't been for a long time. Maybe I didn't even know what "feeling okay" felt like. It's sort of interesting to say it like this. It sounds hopeless, but it was honest and real. That was big for me.

CANDACE: I'm not sure you can have much lower self-esteem than what I had when I got diagnosed with ADHD. I was like a silent anxious mouse cowering in the corner trying not to be seen. I'd put up so many walls around me and had changed the world to suit exactly what I was comfortable doing. I'd lost all ability to act or feel confident or empowered about anything. It was hard to see that though, hidden by the fact I'd molded everything around my fears.

Finding self-worth is one of my biggest challenges and feeds into my social anxiety. But having a label for what I've gone through is a big deal and has been a huge part of getting through this. It makes me feel less alone, less like it's all my fault. It gives me direction to try knocking stuff off. Every little fear I move past makes a difference.

Questions	Priority *(circle one)*	My symptoms of ADHD that affect this area are ...
Do I have a healthy self-esteem level?	*1 - none* *2 - moderate* *3 - high*	
Do I feel that ADHD has gotten in the way of self-awareness?	*1 - none* *2 - moderate* *3 - high*	
Am I hard on myself?	*1 - none* *2 - moderate* *3 - high*	
Do I tend to focus on my weaknesses more than my strengths or successes?	*1 - none* *2 - moderate* *3 - high*	
Do I overestimate my abilities and then create a cycle of disappointment?	*1 - none* *2 - moderate* *3 - high*	

Tip from Dr. Anne: *As you go through this process, remember the difference between self-esteem and self-confidence. We meet many clients who are confident, have big personalities and are seen as strong, powerful personas. Yet, when we get to know these individuals, we realize they're often masking feelings of low self-esteem and self-doubt.*

When you think of self-esteem, think about your inner dialogue and the way you approach decisions and goals. Think about whether you have a clear self-voice and ability to "trust your gut" and believe in yourself. If you have been unknowingly dealing with ADHD symptoms up to this point in your life, it can be challenging to tease apart the layers and get to a place of peace with yourself based on a clear understanding of who you are. Take time with this area of well-being and be as honest as possible with yourself.

ACADEMIC/ OCCUPATIONAL

ADHD symptoms can impact your ability to focus optimally and meet your potential at work or school. That does not mean, however, you can't be successful. The more you know about how your brain works, the more you can control how well you do. Finding the right type of learning environment or workplace and, perhaps more importantly, identifying topics or types of work that engage your brain are essential for optimizing your strengths and talents.

Perhaps you're a surgeon who can't keep up with your paperwork, or a writer who can't write until the last minute, or a CEO who struggles without the support of an administrative assistant. Usually, when ADHD is untreated, work or school is one of the first areas affected. In many cases, the issue is one of imbalance, where the coping mechanisms you need to do well in one area create suffering or problems in another. Perhaps you excel at your job, but it comes at a cost, to the detriment of other areas.

SUSTAINING FOCUS

We know a diagnosis of ADHD doesn't mean you can't focus. It means that you struggle with regulating your focus. This is an important distinction. When it comes to work or school, maintaining focus can feel unpredictable. When will I be able to engage and get this done? When will my brain inevitably let me down?

Think beyond whether you have focusing problems. Instead, explore specifically what "blocks" you. Maybe it feels like your brain gives up before you even start. Or knowing a big task is coming up sets off your anxiety. What is your inner dialogue when trying to get a task done? The more you understand what helps or hinders your focus in daily tasks, the easier it will be to find solutions. Learning how to trust that your brain will do what you need it to do when you need it takes a lot of trial and error (and creative thinking).

TIM: Work was an escape. I didn't want to come home, and didn't know how to be present with my family, so work gave me a good excuse. The culture of being a lawyer made it easy in that I didn't see myself as having a choice. You often need to work late whether you were productive with your day or not. I was doing such a bad job at home as a father and husband that I kept staying late and focusing on providing financially instead.

I had so much trouble getting into things at the beginning of the day though. I'd stay late to make up for it, which justified having slower mornings. My job also involves a ton of reading, and I have to be on top of things when reviewing contracts. That takes a lot of focus for anyone, let alone someone with ADHD. So, as you can imagine, my nights and weekends were filled with work. In retrospect, I was working in short bursts of focus, which some experts recommend, but it wasn't by choice.

AMY: It's funny being asked if you can maintain focus when you have untreated ADHD. Of course not, but could I see that then? And what could I do about it anyway? I mean, I know what you're getting at. The short answer is that I am productive but I do things in a way that works for me, and the process is all pretty unpredictable. I guess that's why I got into personal training in the first place. It was here where my energy and spontaneity could actually be advantageous. Being late all the time, though, and not properly keeping track of my clients' progress and workout preferences eventually impacted how well they were doing. So, I see now how much my focusing challenges affected my work, even if I could laugh it off with clients in the moment.

Now that I see things differently, I can be much more strategic and efficient. I no longer accept being late or not following through for myself or others. I have more structure and routines, which gives me some control. I actually feel like I can trust that my brain will be there when I need it. I have come such a long way.

Questions	Priority (circle one)	My symptoms of ADHD that affect this area are ...
Are there times when I can focus better than others?	1 - none 2 - moderate 3 - high	
Do I hyper-focus on activities?	1 - none 2 - moderate 3 - high	
Am I easily distracted?	1 - none 2 - moderate 3 - high	
When do I find it most difficult to manage distractions or maintain focus?	1 - none 2 - moderate 3 - high	

Tip from Coach Laura: *Many of the adults we see have become so accustomed to having to work around ADHD symptoms that they can't imagine their brain could work another way. Perhaps they wait until midnight the night before a paper is due, and then describe feeling like they were "hit by lightning" and suddenly able to get their work done. "That's when I do my best work" is an assertion we've heard many times.*

Ask yourself, "Are there costs involved with this last-minute style of work?" In most cases, after reflecting on this question, clients see there are impacts to themselves and/or their loved ones and realize they want to live differently.

It can be very stressful and passive-feeling to wait until a rush of adrenaline takes over. Gaining more control and predictability over your focus and productivity can make a huge difference for your overall well-being and your close relationships. Remember: how you feel about your ability to focus will influence your ability to actually do it.

DELEGATION

Delegation requires a lot of planning. You must understand how you want the project to look and give team members adequate notice and building blocks to succeed independently. You also want to avoid the pitfall of delegating simply out of duress. Delegation should be about harnessing, building and using people's skill sets, not having your team help do the job you should have done before it became last-minute. For individuals with ADHD, all this can be challenging.

If ADHD symptoms aren't being managed, delegation at work can be particularly problematic. To help set you (and your team) up to win, investigate what symptoms impact your ability to stay organized and keep track of timelines and develop some strategies to address them. For example, techniques like mini-deadlines with team accountability can optimize productivity. Or working closely with others from the start can reduce symptoms of procrastination or difficulties "chunking up" the project into manageable steps.

CANDACE: I've always seen work as a solitary thing, so I've just done it alone. When I was younger, I was the kid who was happy to do the whole project for the group, and they could just put their names on it. That way, I wouldn't have to face any social conflict, and I knew it was done to my standards. I could also do it on my own time — it's not like I had plans anyway.

All my life, I've worked away in the corner, overcompensating for when I can't focus and making sure I get it done ... no matter the cost. I really haven't learned how to work with others, but now that I understand why, it's an area I'm trying to navigate. Better late than never!

TIM: For most of my career, I had no idea how to properly delegate. I just didn't see it ... I didn't have the perspective, I guess. First of all, I didn't want anyone to see how last-minute I was doing everything, so letting anyone in (even a junior) wasn't an option. Secondly, I didn't know how to chunk up any tasks, because I always did everything in one final "swoop" at the end.

Once I came to realize these "blockers" and started to use the administrative support I had at my disposal, everything changed. Work became more social, less stressful. The biggest weight was lifted when I didn't have to hide anymore. I was good at my job, but that didn't mean I had to do everything by myself in the middle of the night.

Questions	Priority (circle one)	My symptoms of ADHD that affect this area are ...
Do I underestimate or overestimate how long tasks will take?	1 - none 2 - moderate 3 - high	
Do I take on too much or not enough?	1 - none 2 - moderate 3 - high	
Do I get things done on time?	1 - none 2 - moderate 3 - high	
Do I work well with group members?	1 - none 2 - moderate 3 - high	

Tip from Dr. Anne: *Figuring out whether you can delegate differently, or more strategically, can be a challenging process that requires introspection, maybe a whiteboard and ideally a friend or coach to bounce ideas off of. At first, you may think you're already delegating as effectively as possible, but there's almost always room for creative thinking and collaboration in this area.*

We get stuck in patterns. When undiagnosed ADHD has been in the picture, reflecting on this area can be a real game-changer. Ask yourself, "Am I making choices that are rooted in habit or truly bringing out my strengths or the strengths of others?" Improving delegation skills can translate to smarter work, which leads to better results.

MEETING DEADLINES

Untreated ADHD can hold you back from getting things done well by their deadlines. Sometimes, meeting a project due date happens at the cost of other parts of your life. In many cases, it can become a significant performance issue at work or school. Even if a task does get done, many of our clients are left asking "If I'd started earlier, could I have done better?" or thinking "It went well considering I did it all the night before."

Feelings of anxiety and stress may indeed hold you back from creating your absolute best work, but that sense of urgency can also propel you to finally get started, albeit at the last minute. Learning how to get work done as part of a process can be one of the most meaningful areas of behavior change.

JASON: Getting things done became impossible. When football season was on, I had help from the team tutor, and during first semester, I was holding it together. I guess it was because I didn't want to let the team or my coach down, and somehow I would get it together just in time.

By the next semester though, things spiraled. I wouldn't get projects done until the last minute, and then there were too many other things I hadn't done in the meantime. I couldn't try anymore. The readings added up, and the projects were so big. I couldn't see a way through, and it all became too much. That's when I essentially gave up and started to think there was something wrong with me.

AMY: Oh, I had an excuse for everything. I technically had the time, but I still couldn't get anything done. I'd pull it off with all-nighters during school. I still don't know how I got through my work those nights. I guess I was so scared of getting kicked out of school, I just buckled down. It was really unhealthy though, and that style of working only became more stressful once I had more commitments.

When I was doing personal training, I often compensated for being late by going long or giving extra attention in other ways. I would constantly make excuses for why I didn't have the workout fully prepared or was arriving without the proper attire. I didn't realize how much of a pattern it was. I've only been able to see that in retrospect. My clients must have been annoyed or disappointed. I guess they didn't say anything because they didn't want to hurt my feelings. I've apologized to many of them since.

Questions	Priority *(circle one)*	My symptoms of ADHD that affect this area are ...
Do I avoid or put off finishing tasks?	1 - none 2 - moderate 3 - high	
Do I lose interest or get distracted before a project is completed?	1 - none 2 - moderate 3 - high	
Do I struggle with completing tasks because I get distracted by another idea or to-do?	1 - none 2 - moderate 3 - high	
Am I unsure how to start a task?	1 - none 2 - moderate 3 - high	

Tip from Dr. Anne: *By changing how you feel about tasks and learning new ways to manage your work process, you can change the way your brain responds to upcoming tasks. If you're always waiting for a "burst of neurotransmitters" because a deadline is looming, or because you've run out of distractions or excuses, you and your brain have created a pattern where you don't feel you can start until you get that burst.*

Learn a more balanced process to help you stay engaged through to the end. Completing tasks requires a new outlook and cognitive reframing. Remember neuroplasticity? You can teach your brain a new trick or two. And it's exciting when you feel you're completing something to the best of your ability — and starting earlier than the old you might have.

PUNCTUALITY

For people with strong, consistent executive functions, making plans, being prepared and leaving a buffer to ensure timeliness can all come easily. When you have ADHD though, many of the conventional systems for keeping track of time and managing priorities do not work well.

Often when an individual has untreated ADHD, they've grown so accustomed to being late and arriving without the necessary materials that they're stuck living in stressful patterns of continually rushing and letting themselves and others down. These patterns can become cyclical, cementing feelings of defensiveness as they try to explain themselves to those they've disappointed.

JASON: I'm starting to apply what I've learned about myself to actual changes with life stuff. It's all been so much to take in, to breathe through and face. I've had to spend a lot of time just learning to be, without pushing myself to do everything at once. So, in that sense, I'm still late for everything. I haven't been able to make a lot of tangible progress with stuff like being on time or organized.

What has changed is that I see it differently now. I see why I've always been late. I've also become comfortable asking for help. I know this sounds basic, but I'll even chat out the steps to getting somewhere with a friend. I think I'm getting closer, at least I feel like I'm getting there.

TIM: When things were at their worst, I could blame anyone for anything. It was never my fault when I was late for dinner. I never even had the courtesy to tell Jane I was going to be late in the first place.

The most interesting thing to me now is that I never thought it was my fault. I didn't see the pattern. Every time it happened, I had a reason or a viable excuse, even if others would say, "Oh that's so Tim." I honestly thought life was getting in my way. I'm not saying I'm on time now, but I'm way more aware of my actions, and way better at admitting where I had a role. It means I can have a dialogue about it and acknowledge my contributions.

Questions	Priority (circle one)	My symptoms of ADHD that affect this area are ...
Do I lose track of belongings?	*1 - none* *2 - moderate* *3 - high*	
Do I have difficulty remembering tasks, dates and appointments?	*1 - none* *2 - moderate* *3 - high*	
Do I have any organizational systems in place to help manage forgetfulness?	*1 - none* *2 - moderate* *3 - high*	
Can I keep track of time?	*1 - none* *2 - moderate* *3 - high*	
How do I manage my paper work? What does my desk, office, room, home, etc. look like?	*1 - none* *2 - moderate* *3 - high*	

Tip from Dr. Anne: *Many Springboard clients need to learn to take responsibility for shortcomings (or symptoms) that affect themselves and their loved ones. Even if it feels like "it was the fault of traffic" or the result of an unpredictable event, it's important to take responsibility for actions that impact others.*

Clients going through ADHD treatment often have to learn strategies like working backward to sort out timing or building in time for error or unforeseen issues. Outsmart yourself and anticipate you will be running late. When planning, don't depend on the best-case scenario. Being realistic will decrease stress. This type of strategy does not usually come naturally for individuals with ADHD — it takes time and hard work to break old patterns.

ADMINISTRATIVE TASKS

Nowadays, we all have a huge number of administrative tasks to keep up with. Getting groceries, renewing your license, staying on track with taxes, reporting or tracking systems in your workplace — there's more administrative work and paperwork than ever. And with so many competing priorities, it's more challenging to stay on track.

When ADHD is in the picture, these to-dos are compounded by struggles with completing detailed steps in the right order, multitasking and prioritizing responsibilities. It's no wonder many people with ADHD find themselves unable to stay on track with important duties and then get so far behind that it feels unmanageable. When you're behind on parking tickets, taxes or credit card bills, it's not only stressful, but can have real consequences.

CANDACE: I tend to be careful and afraid of doing something "wrong," so that's helped me stay on top of my administrative responsibilities pretty much across the board. I'm not in debt, for example, and I'm not late on my taxes or anything. But there's one big skeleton in my closet: I've been so bad about submitting expenses at work. My company probably owes me thousands of dollars from over the years. I was always running late on it, and then felt embarrassed, and then wasn't sure exactly how to do it properly. So I have just not submitted the receipts. I have traveled to conferences, even bought a new laptop — and never asked for the money back. It's pretty embarrassing admitting this out loud. It sounds so irresponsible. This is something I am going to face and fix — at least for my out-of-pocket expenses this year.

AMY: I've been building systems that work better for me to keep on top of all my paperwork. I'm trying to focus on three things a day and not get sidetracked with new priorities. I'm getting better at completing my kids' school forms, sticking to meal planning and working on systems that help our whole family stay on track. Some changes have been easier than I thought and that's been great. I'm realizing how hard it was to be around me. I was like a spinning top. Now, I feel like I'm spinning more slowly and intentionally picking my direction.

Questions	Priority (circle one)	My symptoms of ADHD that affect this area are ...
Do I have balance with my competing responsibilities (for example, career, school, parenting, household tasks, well-being)? Does one suffer more than another?	1 - none 2 - moderate 3 - high	
Do I have ways to manage competing responsibilities?	1 - none 2 - moderate 3 - high	
Do I know how to prioritize what needs to get done?	1 - none 2 - moderate 3 - high	
Do I have strategies when I need to get administrative tasks done (for example, taxes)?	1 - none 2 - moderate 3 - high	

Tip from Coach Laura: *When it comes to managing administrative tasks, we see three areas that can be problematic for people with ADHD.*

First, people often don't get help until it's such a huge problem that it requires almost a heroic effort to get resolved. For example, taxes that haven't been filed for years, or debilitating credit card debt. Of course, it can be hard to ask for help, maybe because it feels embarrassing or overwhelming. But if you can notice the problems and get support in place sooner, this can avoid a major long-term problem.

Another situation we often see is people managing administrative tasks with a system that doesn't work for their brain style. Trying to do things the way a more linear thinker would do it can make a task even more unmanageable and unsustainable. Determining a process that works for how you work can help you make more effective systems.

Lastly, people are hesitant to get help, convincing themselves they can do it on their own. But if you're facing an ongoing task you know will be a struggle, we recommend getting support. Outsource where possible: set up automatic bill payments, meet monthly with an organizer or arrange for administrative support. Don't be afraid to get help and bear the cost. In the long run, the alternative is almost always more stressful — and often more expensive.

WHERE TO GO FROM HERE?

We know that going through the process of assessing the ways in which attention issues impact your life can be challenging. For some, it's an overwhelming journey. It may feel tedious or repetitive, like a giant to-do list.

Remember this chapter's two primary goals: to help you think more about where ADHD affects your life, and to identify your strengths and goals for change by exploring your overall health. By taking a snapshot of right now, you can begin to move forward.

The tough news? ADHD usually impacts more areas than you think. The good news? Treating ADHD can have huge effects in all areas of your life. Even more good news? When you make a change in one area, even something small, it can have spillover effects into other areas, motivating further change and creating a snowball effect. And remember what you learned about brain function and the effects of neuroplasticity: by shifting the way you approach your goals and tasks, you can actually change the way your brain works.

This is your opportunity to see yourself differently, look at your shortcomings — and strengths — through a new lens and start to truly manage your symptoms of ADHD.

WHAT HAVE YOU LEARNED IN THIS CHAPTER?
WHAT DO YOU NOW KNOW ABOUT YOUR HEALTH AND ADHD?

CHAPTER 5

TAKE THE LEAD WITH ADHD

Now that you know more about your symptoms of ADHD and how your brain functions and you've evaluated the areas of your life you'd like to improve, it's time to take back control.

It's time to take the lead with your ADHD.

This phase starts with you deciding which areas are priorities. For many reasons, we encourage our clients to take time to reflect on this before moving forward too quickly with an action plan.

One of the main reasons is that when an ADHD-style brain is alert and engaged, executive function challenges are less problematic. Therefore, following through on your own intentions becomes easier. On the other hand, when there's no sense of urgency — in other words, it's a less personal interest or there's no short-term reward — associated with a task, follow-through may be challenging. In essence, it can be difficult to "fake it" with your executive functions. They either wake up or fall asleep depending on a complicated balance of interests/rewards/motivations.

Another reason we suggest pausing is based on something we often hear our clients talk about: they feel like they've been spinning their wheels for most of their lives. They've been so busy trying to meet expectations that they've rarely stopped to ask themselves where their motivation lies or why something is important to them. Sometimes it turns out not to be important! For example, you say you want or need to do something, but you actually don't want or need to do it at all. Yet it weighs on you — you feel it's something you're "supposed" to do.

So before beginning to make changes, assess what you really, truly want. That can be harder to figure out than it sounds, so be patient.

ARE MY PRIORITIES WANTS, NEEDS OR SHOULDS?

Like an onion, your diagnosis has many layers. This process is about peeling back those layers and taking small, manageable steps toward your goals. Once you separate your wants and needs from your shoulds, you can develop strategies that enable you to take more control of your ADHD and follow through on your intentions with appropriate actions. Check off the areas you identified as a high priority for change in chapter 4 starting on page 73. Then decide whether each is a want, a need or a should.

Health domain	High priority for change?	Want, need or should? (circle one)		
PHYSICAL	☐ Sleep	Want	Need	Should
	☐ Nutrition	Want	Need	Should
	☐ Physical activity	Want	Need	Should
	☐ Substance use	Want	Need	Should
	☐ Screen use	Want	Need	Should
SOCIAL	☐ Home life routines	Want	Need	Should
	☐ Money management	Want	Need	Should
	☐ Driving awareness	Want	Need	Should
	☐ Communication	Want	Need	Should
	☐ Relationships	Want	Need	Should
	☐ Physical intimacy/sex	Want	Need	Should
EMOTIONAL	☐ Stress management	Want	Need	Should
	☐ Anger management	Want	Need	Should
	☐ Healthy outlet expression	Want	Need	Should
	☐ Connecting with others	Want	Need	Should
	☐ Self-esteem maintenance	Want	Need	Should
ACADEMIC/ OCCUPATIONAL	☐ Sustaining focus	Want	Need	Should
	☐ Delegation	Want	Need	Should
	☐ Meeting deadlines	Want	Need	Should
	☐ Punctuality	Want	Need	Should
	☐ Administrative tasks	Want	Need	Should

First, let's deal with the shoulds. Of all the areas rated as priorities, the shoulds are typically the most challenging for those with ADHD. Not because people don't want to make progress, but because, when it comes to tasks in the should category, their neurotransmitters aren't going to support access to the parts of the brain in charge of motivation and executive functions. This means you're trying to improve these areas using sheer will, grit and tears or, if you're more self-aware, through creative thinking and external supports.

Understanding the root of the "should emotion" can help sort out what competing voices may be part of the dialogue. Whose voice is telling you that you "should" do this? Yours or someone else's? Is it a helpful voice? Or is that "should" better framed as a want or a need? Doing something because you think you *should* is not very inspiring.

Before you begin to work on action steps, it's important to own your genuine wants and needs.

BREAKING DOWN MY SHOULDS

Choose all shoulds from the previous activity and take a closer look at them.

My should	Who says so?	Is this really *my* priority for change?	Can I reframe it into a want or need?	Action step

Having explored any shoulds in this activity, you are left with your wants and needs. Now we're getting to the root of where *you* are actually motivated to make changes. The challenge is to avoid making an unrealistic goal by having too big of a change too fast.

The most successful way to make long-term behavior change is to start with small, consistent, sustainable steps. Just like walking the dog every morning before work is a good step toward building physical activity into your life, start with small nudges that can become patterns in your life.

PARING DOWN MY GOALS

Look at your priorities for change in the activity on page 125, and ask yourself what would help improve each area. Record these goals in the first column. Now make each goal smaller ... and smaller ... and mini-tweak it. Our example shows you how it works.

This activity prompts you to take a Plan A and break it into more practical, manageable steps. This can help you avoid setting a goal that's too big of a change, setting you up for frustration and disappointment. Even if you're doing a small step, you still feel good about progress and hold momentum. Learning habits is hard stuff!

The goal	Now make it smaller ...	... smaller ...	... and mini-tweak
Get to the gym every day	Get to the gym twice a week, and work out 20 minutes at home other days	Get to the gym once a week, and work out at home twice a week	Walk the dog every morning and take the stairs at the office

Tip from Dr. Anne: As you set your goals, make sure each is a SMART goal. Introduced by George Doran in 1981, "SMART" commonly stands for specific, measurable, achievable, relevant and time-bound. It's a good way for people with ADHD to make sure they aren't falling into that old trap of setting unrealistic or unattainable goals, and then beating themselves up for falling short.

This is a good time to talk about one of the fundamental concepts of our coaching programs: the recurring disconnect between intentions and desired outcomes. Even if an individual cares and wants to do something, their executive functions let them down and they're unable to meet their expectations. If this becomes a pattern, they get frustrated, and the more frustrated they get, the more blocked they get (both consciously and unconsciously).

In coaching sessions, our clients set their intentions, but we help them find ways to think outside the box about what strategies would help them get to where they want. We spend a lot of time meticulously "walking through" what has stopped them in the past, so we can find ways to follow through successfully.

Time management, in particular, often gets in the way of transitioning from an intention into an action. Many clients with ADHD describe having good intentions and truly planning to "get everything done" or "get there on time," but struggle with accurately estimating time or making realistic plans. So being aware of how good you are at judging time is essential to goal setting.

HOW AM I AT JUDGING TIME?

Pick a few everyday tasks, estimate how long they'll take you and identify obstacles that might get in the way of completing them. Time the tasks as you do them, then see how close you were.

   Understanding where you underestimate or overestimate time can help you become more aware of how you manage your time and provide necessary data when you get serious about turning your intentions into actions.

Task	I think it will take …	What could get in the way?	It actually took me …	What have I learned?

Time management is one possible barrier to turning an intention into an action, but there are many others. We use the term "blocker" at Springboard Clinic because it captures the feeling our clients have when pursuing their intentions — they often get blocked or stuck. Blockers can be tricky to identify. They can be real, they can be perceived, or they can be symptoms of ADHD. If you want more success with meeting goals, even small ones, understanding your blockers is a good place to start.

What's *really* getting in the way? It might be something so small, or it could be something enormous. The workaround to your blocker might be as easy as having your gym clothes in the car or making a deal with a friend that you'll take the stairs. In contrast, your blocker could be something bigger, like not feeling comfortable in a gym setting. In that case, consider going with a friend, changing which gym you belong to or working out at home. By taking the time to reflect on what's stopping you, you can modify your action plans and more accurately target solutions.

Tip from Coach Laura: *It's not uncommon for someone to come to a coaching session and say, "I failed. I didn't do my goals." From the coaching perspective, I'm sorry my client is disappointed, but it's the jumping-off point I'm looking for. We then start a process of digging deep, exploring what nuances and themes got in the way. We spend time getting into the minutiae, because that's often where the answer is. It's in this work that our clients really learn about their own brains: what drives them and what holds them back.*

This type of self-discovery is always time well spent. Don't be afraid of failing as you make new goals. The process of digging deep about "the why" will guide your self-reflection, and ultimately help you follow through more reliably.

IDENTIFYING MY BLOCKERS

It's time to be honest about what will likely stop you from meeting your intentions.

First, check out the example on the next page of a "blocker sheet" filled out by Jason. His goal is to put in his school application. As you can see, there are both real and perceived blockers that will nag at him. It is also worth noting he's included a Plan B (which involves seeking help), if he's not able to meet his Plan A.

After you've seen how Jason would tackle his blockers, turn to pages 134 and 135. Pick two "mini-tweaks" from "Paring down my goals" on page 128. Fill out the sheets to see how you could approach potential blockers.

Be as honest as possible about what might get in the way. For example, instead of saying "I'll be too lazy," dig in and think about your internal dialogue, watching for familiar patterns. Ask yourself *exactly* what you think will get in the way of following through. Is it that you'll forget, or think you'll do it tomorrow instead, or that you need a more urgent deadline? As we often say with clients, "Try to get weirdly specific!"

Fill out both Plan A and B. Behavior-change goals usually don't go as planned, so being prepared with another solution can be a good motivational tool. This way, you can see progress one way or the other.

This activity helps you cognitively assess the steps from an intention all the way through to an action. It's the best way we know to set you up to outsmart your ADHD symptoms.

WHAT IS MY GOAL?

Get my application submitted to return to school

WHAT MIGHT BLOCK ME FROM ATTAINING IT?

Confusion, frustration, not knowing which forms to complete, or who to send it to, shame, distraction, procrastination

WHICH OF THESE BLOCKERS ARE PERCEIVED?

Frustration
Shame
Distraction
Procrastination

WHICH OF THESE BLOCKERS ARE REAL?

Confusion
Not knowing how to do it

WHAT ARE SOME STRATEGIES TO MANAGE THESE BLOCKERS?

Motivational journaling, listening to pump-up music, chunking it up, take breaks

WHAT CAN I DO TO OVERCOME THESE BLOCKERS?

Ask someone from the school to walk me through it, Look over their website to find out what I need to do

ACTION PLAN A: Monday morning, set myself up with music, at a coffee shop, and look at the website — don't leave until I've figured out my steps.

ACTION PLAN B: Tuesday morning, ask one of my parents to help me navigate the website to figure out the steps.

WHAT IS MY GOAL?

WHAT MIGHT BLOCK ME FROM ATTAINING IT?

WHICH OF THESE BLOCKERS ARE PERCEIVED?

WHICH OF THESE BLOCKERS ARE REAL?

WHAT ARE SOME STRATEGIES TO MANAGE THESE BLOCKERS?

WHAT CAN I DO TO OVERCOME THESE BLOCKERS?

ACTION PLAN A:

ACTION PLAN B:

WHAT IS MY GOAL?

WHAT MIGHT BLOCK ME FROM ATTAINING IT?

WHICH OF THESE BLOCKERS ARE PERCEIVED?

WHICH OF THESE BLOCKERS ARE REAL?

WHAT ARE SOME STRATEGIES TO MANAGE THESE BLOCKERS?

WHAT CAN I DO TO OVERCOME THESE BLOCKERS?

ACTION PLAN A:

ACTION PLAN B:

HOW DID LEARNING ABOUT BLOCKERS HELP YOU BEAT ADHD?

At Springboard, we know clients are making progress when they start using the term "blockers" naturally. They arrive at a session, and instead of being frustrated about mistakes, they jump right into telling us what got in their way over the week. They walk us through what held them back and what they need to do to get back on track.

Let's see what our group members experienced once they identified their blockers.

JASON: When I started to face my diagnosis with an honest lens, all I could see were blockers. Everywhere. I'd hit a wall in so many areas of my life and was faced with hurdles I couldn't even name. It was like I was in a pressure cooker and I had all these things I was supposed to do but no idea how to do them. I didn't know where to begin.

I had to work hard to figure out what I wanted to do, even down to what I wanted for breakfast. It was like the very fabric of who I was didn't feel like me. That was the hard part. Once I knew what I truly wanted for myself, I started to tick off steps. I could start to beat ADHD a little bit at a time. Then the real motivation kicked in. As my goals felt more like mine, I was able to set a true intention and actually follow through.

CANDACE: Being honest about what was really blocking me was complicated. I'd been living with avoidance and anxiety for so long, I didn't know how to tease apart what was what. What was something I didn't like doing vs. something I was scared to mess up? I had to figure out where that line was and carefully and consciously identify my goals so I could identify what I actually wanted and needed.

I realized early though that I wanted more connection in my life. I wanted to stop protecting myself, to recognize all the voices in my head and instead trust my own. I wanted to try to live a little and take even a small risk. That was the best-case scenario. Joy and fun weren't even in the conversation.

TIM: Post-diagnosis, everything changed. It was like once the blindfold was taken off and I really saw who I'd become, I felt as if I had a second chance. I had to work hard at getting past my anger and defensiveness, but once I could see through those emotions, I could start to see all the little things that were blocking me. The decisions and changes I made from there became almost easy. I mean, obviously the symptoms of ADHD were still there, but I could see them and tackle them without all the layers.

For me, the tough thing to deal with wasn't the symptoms themselves, it was all the baggage I carried around to cope with them. That's what was so isolating. And confounding. I had to work hard to see that, but moving forward has been a relief and the actual steps have gone relatively smoothly.

AMY: I eventually figured out that what was blocking me from doing what I actually wanted were mostly micro things. I was this chicken running around with my head cut off, with no particular plan or direction, all under the guise of being productive and doing everything for everyone.

My path to transformation was all in the micros, the smallest little blockers that were getting in the way and their obvious mini-solutions. Like the voice that said, "I'm not going to the gym because I need two hours." I *know* better. I know that even 20 minutes will help me. I need to keep running shoes in the car so I can grab a run when I drop the kids off.

A STORY FROM COACH LAURA:
LEARNING TO FORGIVE YOURSELF

So many of my clients set unrealistic and overwhelming to-do lists for themselves. And so entrenched are these undoable lists that it's no surprise people get down on themselves.

I was once working with a woman in her 40s, a dynamic individual with two children, a busy job and a wonderful upbeat energy. For all intents and purposes, she had it all. But as we worked through her day-to-day, she shared her inner sadness. She was going through the motions but felt empty inside. She was doing everything and yet nothing.

This client's shame and guilt were so deeply ingrained in her thought patterns that she essentially always felt like she never measured up. When she failed, even if it was small — such as being a few minutes late for picking up the kids or not having a healthy enough meal prepped for her family — she'd beat herself up. She'd be openly frustrated with her family and then get even more stuck in a cycle of guilt and shame. Often "upset about being upset," she'd find herself in a dark cloud of her own feelings. Her husband was supportive and caring, but she couldn't hear his words, she had such deep-seated negative self-talk.

As she and I explored these stormy thoughts, she realized she was the one who put herself in that state — and she'd also have to be the one who set herself free. One day, I wrote "Forgiveness is a gift to the self" on the whiteboard. She and I stared at it for a while and then made eye contact. "I have to forgive myself, don't I?" She said. She had to learn how to cut herself some slack, let go, stop getting stuck in her own feelings of who she *should* be and ... just be. She had to learn how to put down her defenses, disassemble the walls she'd built around her and let herself make mistakes, without punishing herself and pulling away.

WHAT HAVE YOU LEARNED IN THIS CHAPTER?
WHAT DO YOU NOW KNOW ABOUT TAKING THE LEAD WITH ADHD?

CHAPTER 6:

YOU ARE NOT YOUR ADHD

As you learn to close the gap between your intentions and your actions, you'll gain confidence and trust in yourself. You'll begin to differentiate your sense of self from the ADHD symptoms you experience. And by treating your ADHD as a third party, you can neutralize it. You can define it, accept it, understand it and make it impersonal. From there, you can separate yourself from your ADHD and begin to talk openly with others about it. We want to empower you to break down the walls you may have surrounded yourself with and, with them, the way they make you feel.

As a result of the work you've done, we hope you're more comfortable with and accepting of your symptoms. Now that you've identified how they affect your life and learned how to set goals to stay on track in an ADHD-friendly way, you're ready to get real with your ADHD.

Tip from Dr. Anne: Whenever my clients talk about how they view and describe themselves, they inevitably say something like, "Well, it might be hard to believe but I care a lot about X, even though my actions don't always send that message." We could be discussing parenting, relationships, work, personal responsibilities or simply responding to an email from an old friend — anytime the client's feelings or intentions do not match up with what they actually do. This is confusing for them, and can create hurt and frustration in their relationships.

Our clients and those around them often struggle to define their intentions and separate them from their actions. By sharing more about your desired actions with those close to you, you can help reduce your negative thought patterns and any "extra baggage" you may be carrying. Learning to communicate — first with yourself, then with those impacted by you — is an important step to feeling more connected and understood.

There are many common misinterpretations of symptoms of ADHD. For example, if someone is running late to meet you, it might be easy to assume your meeting isn't important to them, or *you* aren't important to them. But at Springboard Clinic, when our clients run late, we don't take it personally and think, "Well, they obviously don't want to come to this appointment." They were the ones who booked it!

Because we know our clients struggle with time management, we know their symptoms have gotten in the way and that their tardiness isn't a value judgment on the appointment. It doesn't mean there aren't consequences for this, but it does mean, as clinicians, we don't get offended or take it personally.

Unfortunately, not everybody in our clients' lives have the benefit of those insights. While many people come to us with strong support from a spouse or parent, others have lost relationships. Adults with ADHD have often hit a low point before they finally reach out for help, typically in their personal life, but it can be in career as well.

Many of our clients spend their days oscillating between being caught up in the moment and stressed out because they're running late. It's not a fun way to spend a day. And it can be a tough cycle to break. By the time we meet our clients, they've spent a large part of their life defending themselves against all the suggestions of shoulds, reminders of to-dos, criticisms, nagging and frustration from others.

Working through the denial of symptoms and toward acceptance is key to figuring out how to live with your symptoms of ADHD. The process of learning to neutralize and depersonalize ADHD symptoms starts with you, but this same process becomes important for those close to you as well. This joint strategy can help you get to the root of issues affecting you and your crew.

Tip from Dr. Anne: When I offer clients a reminder email summarizing our session together and they reply confidently "No need — I'll remember this!" I know we may have to step back and work on accepting and understanding their symptoms of ADHD. Similarly, when they reschedule and don't mark it in their calendar or ask for a reminder email, I often take the opportunity to ask a few follow-up questions. I want to make sure they're continuing to become more self-aware, honest and open about where symptoms might get in the way. "Know thyself"— there's a lot of power in that.

Self-acceptance is important in everyone's life, but for adults with ADHD — given their history of having to defend themselves and prove to others (and themselves) that they can follow through — self-acceptance can be a challenging prospect. It's almost as if, by asking for that reminder email (even if it's from their ADHD coach), they're proving all their critics right. So be willing to be vigilant, honest and vulnerable when it comes to accepting your symptoms. This will help you avoid conflating your symptoms of ADHD with your sense of self.

Here's the thing: if you want to live with your ADHD in the best way possible, it's important to be honest about your track record. ADHD is not who you are, your self-worth or even why people appreciate you. But facing the truth about how your symptoms affect others is a huge part of "making your diagnosis neutral" in your life.

This can help you avoid defensive behaviors, which are often the root of conflict. If you can acknowledge when and why you're forgetful, disorganized or frequently late, do things last-minute, talk a lot and have trouble doing certain tasks, you can apologize without feeling like your whole self-worth has been compromised.

At the same time, the underlying goal is to work toward implementing compensatory strategies or ways to make the next situation different. At Springboard Clinic, we encourage our clients to sift through their past, be honest with themselves about their abilities (including symptoms of ADHD) and work toward changing their future.

This might sound complicated, but it's our experience that when you reduce the negative secondary symptoms you experience, you can save energy for managing the actual symptoms, which can yield effective results faster.

ADHD AND DEFENSIVENESS

When you have ADHD, you've likely become used to struggling to follow through on things (simple or complex), even when you really want to do them. You've probably always felt that gap between what you want to do and what you actually do. Everyone's story is different, but almost every client we've met describes that feeling.

Perhaps you first felt the gap in grade 2, when you had trouble listening to your teacher and kept getting caught looking out the window. Or maybe it wasn't until grade 7, when you started to realize you couldn't get things done the way your classmates did. Either way, by the time you were a teenager, you'd probably heard more than once, "If only you would put in a better effort and attitude, you'd be a better student."

The problem with this type of narrative is that you start to believe it *is* all your fault. You want to do the right thing, but you keep disappointing yourself and others. So you have to defend yourself. You come up with excuses, and you develop a sensitivity to triggers that make you feel like you're doing it all intentionally or, even worse, maliciously. Instead of getting to the root of the issue, you're focused on the emotional triggers and defending your worth, instead of sorting out what you need to meet both your own and others' expectations. These secondary emotions take up a lot of bandwidth, creating a divide between the individual and his/her support people.

To move away from conflating ADHD with your identity, try to become more aware of these emotional triggers and reactions, so you can set them aside and focus on the best way for you to move forward.

GETTING ON THE DEFENSE

Let's learn more about whether you have feelings of defensiveness and, if so, how they might be impeding your moving forward.

   Complete the following sentences and note any reactive feelings or observations this exercise triggers. If you're going to rally all your energy to fight ADHD, you must understand your ADHD baggage and how you spend your emotional energy.

I first felt like I had to defend myself when _____.

I react really quickly when someone close to me says _____.

The most hurtful comment I remember from when I was younger was

_____.

I wish I could _____ like others seem to be able to do.

I get really stuck when _____.

My insecure, childlike voice comes out when _____.

The part of me that I most want to be different is _____.

I have trouble apologizing when _____.

If one thing could be easier for me, I wish _____.

If I were to let my guard down emotionally, I _____.

WHAT DID YOUR BOXING GLOVES LOOK LIKE?

Let's hear our group members' experiences with getting on the defensive — and what their boxing gloves looked like.

 **JASON:** I'm not a confrontational person — I'll basically do anything to avoid a fight. Occasionally, I got angry and lashed out, especially when I was really disappointed in myself. But most of the time, I'd either pretend not to care or make some self-deprecating joke, criticizing myself before someone else had the chance. I think by doing that, by making myself the joke, I kept everyone at arm's length, didn't let anyone in. I was distant from my own true feelings and those that cared about me. This made it confusing when I worked to get better. But realizing it was big.

CANDACE: I didn't have boxing gloves — I wasn't even in the ring. I was hiding behind my self-made barricade, spending most of my time convincing myself (and anyone who'd listen) that that was where I belonged. My defensiveness could be seen in the way I retreated, in the way I tried to control, in the way I cornered myself. I defended against what I couldn't control and learned how to say no to almost everything. I only put myself in situations that had zero risk to me. That's how I held my ground.

TIM: I ate, slept and basically took every breath with boxing gloves on. Often on edge, I was always prepared to defend myself. Nothing was ever my fault, and I subconsciously did my best to put it back on Jane. I positioned myself as the one being wronged and closed the door to any real conversation. Eventually, she stopped trying to work things out with me. She pulled away and left me in my own reality.

I realize now that her words (usually truthful ones) were words I'd heard throughout my life, and I jumped to push them back as quickly as I could. I felt like I was proving a point to everyone who had ever doubted me. But mostly I think I was angrily retreating and saying what I needed to say to hide the fact that I had trouble following through, for myself or anyone else in my personal life.

AMY: I was certainly angry inside, I think. I mean, I know, *now*. But back then, I distracted myself constantly. I was usually sort of chipper, but when I started to get overwhelmed or burned out, I'd fire off passive-aggressive comments. I didn't see it at the time. I basically thought I was okay. But there was this part of me that would lash out. Lash out because I wasn't taking care of myself.

You probably now have thoughts about your own baggage, as well as an awareness of some of your triggers. What kinds of situations make you feel triggered or have you donning your boxing gloves?

CHANGING MY INTERNAL DIALOGUE

Let's move into the now with an activity about your internal dialogue. Write down a few scenarios where ADHD symptoms get in the way of your ability to follow through. Note how you tend to react with yourself and those around you. The goal is to start seeing how clear and satisfying communication with yourself and others would be if you can eliminate defensiveness from the inside out. To help you get started, we've provided an example.

Scenario	Symptom	Secondary emotion	My self-talk	My action plan
I often run late for work.	Accurately estimating time is hard for me.	I get defensive and angry about being late and feel anxious about rushing.	I want to get better at being honest with myself about how long things take and become more present mentally.	I want to develop routines so my mornings don't feel so stressful, see if I can feel more predictable and reliable.

REFRAMING ADHD'S IMPACT ON OTHERS

Now that you have a better idea about internal impacts of your emotions related to your ADHD symptoms, let's take it a step further. Using the symptoms you identified in the previous activity, name who they impact (beyond yourself) and think about how you want to change your emotional reaction when you experience them.

This activity is about seeing your symptoms clearly and determining how you want to communicate about them. Remember your ADHD bird on page 60? It might be helpful to harness an image for these!

Symptom	Who else does this affect?	How do I want to think about the interaction differently?	How do I want to act in these situations?
Accurately estimating time is hard for me.	*I'm always late for dinner, which impacts my spouse and children.*	*I want to put more value on my family time. I want to leave the office on time, so I arrive in a better headspace and don't let everyone down.*	*I want to stop making excuses about why I'm late. I want to arrive home ready to be a partner and parent. I want to apologize when I'm late and face the reasons why I got behind.*

NO EXCUSES, NO ANGER

You're now able to name ADHD, stare at it and not jump to defend it. Instead of thinking "I can't do that because of my ADHD," we want you to think "I can't do it *that way* because I have ADHD, but how can I still get it done?"

The goal of this activity is to turn the way you'd like to approach your "classic ADHD" scenarios into specific action plans. By getting out of your head, you'll be able to develop actual steps toward achieving your goals.

Start by jotting down a few typical ADHD scenarios you often find yourself in. Then identify your usual reactions you'd like to ditch and how you'd prefer to approach the situation. Like the blocker sheet activity on page 132, we suggest you create a Plan A and Plan B. This way, you won't get too discouraged or stuck in "black and white" thinking. Having a Plan B helps you remember the importance of thinking differently. We've started you off with an example.

My "classic ADHD"	Emotions I'm not going to waste time on	How I want to approach this scenario	Plan A	Plan B
I often lose track of my things.	*My anger and frustration at myself (often directed at my partner).*	*Be more honest about the fact that I need help with systems and need to care about where I leave my stuff (use visual cues to help).*	*Every time I leave home, stop and think about what I need to take with me. Take a minute and pause.*	*Use visual cues or reminders on my phone to help me stop to think.*

DEAR ADHD ...

Write a letter to your ADHD, sharing your philosophy of how you want to move forward from here. Consider adding points about what you're going to start doing, what pitfalls you're ready to avoid and how you are going to stay present in separating this diagnosis from your self-worth.

DEAR ADHD,

A STORY FROM COACH LAURA:
DON'T SWIM UPSTREAM

A client was working on a filing system for himself. He'd hired a personal organizer to create processes for him, especially with paperwork. The organizer did an incredible job, but the upkeep was clearly going to be the issue. We quickly realized that while the organizer's intricate, detail-oriented system may have been intuitive for a linear-style brain, we needed a system that worked like my client's brain.

His filing system was all set up, with files named and ready for him to put papers in each month. That was the problem. The system required him to sort through all his documents and file them in a dozen files monthly. The hydro bill, child-care receipt, credit cart statement, etc. After we talked about it for a few minutes, the solution came to us. Instead of having a file for each kind of bill, he'd have one file per month.

That was it. The July papers went in the July folder — one month, one folder. It was doable and it worked. Always make sure you're not swimming upstream.

WHAT HAVE YOU LEARNED IN THIS CHAPTER?
WHAT DO YOU NOW KNOW ABOUT YOU VS. YOUR ADHD?

CHAPTER 7:

YOU AND YOUR TEAM

ADHD symptoms can wax and wane. How they affect you depends on what you're trying to do with your time. For example, taking on a new job or bigger responsibilities can make your symptoms harder to manage and actively challenge your coping mechanisms. But having the encouragement of a caring team of family, friends, coworkers and a health support community who understands you can make all the difference in your success.

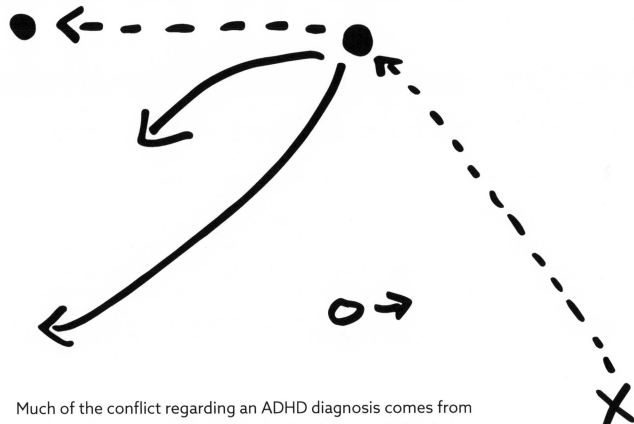

Much of the conflict regarding an ADHD diagnosis comes from secondary issues, such as feelings of guilt, shame or defensiveness, which can lead to breakdowns in communication with others. As you work with your team to speak the same language and develop joint coping mechanisms, you're able to share your true self, get to the root of the issues and ultimately take control of your life.

Many types of professionals can be helpful in supporting adults on their ADHD journey. Medical doctors are one. Others include ADHD coaches, psychologists and support groups specifically for adults with ADHD. Another kind of support is workshops that teach new ways to change a specific area — like procrastination or time management — or learn new skills — like organization, money management or productivity.

When seeking professional help, remember that your relationship with that person will likely have the most influence on your success, so make sure you feel understood, respected and supported. This relationship should ideally translate to increased motivation and participation.

However, not all of our relationships are conducive to helping us in our treatment process. You don't have to tell everyone you know — it's your personal information and your journey. Some people will make you feel good when you share this information, while others may make you feel less positive. This chapter will help you figure out how to navigate these relationships and build your team of supporters.

STARTING TO PICK MY TEAM

Think of the people in your life: those whose words and actions make you feel motivated and accepted, and also those who tend to make you feel more "stuck."

Complete the following statements and see who comes to mind:

_____ is a great listener and support.

_____ often helps me problem-solve tricky situations.

I usually feel better after having vented to _____.

I get into arguments with _____.

I learn new and interesting things when I spend time with _____.

I feel loved and appreciated by _____.

I show my appreciation toward _____.

I usually have a great time with _____.

I don't always feel comfortable around _____.

_____ tends to point out the "silver linings" of my situations.

When I'm feeling down, my first call is usually to _____.

WHAT HAPPENED WHEN YOU SHARED YOUR ADHD DIAGNOSIS WITH OTHERS?

Sharing personal and truly meaningful information about ourselves is never easy. Let's hear a little from our group members about how it was for them.

JASON: Trying to explain ADHD to my parents was really hard. When I told them, they were kind of like, "Okay, so … ?" They didn't believe it was a bigger priority for me than the drinking, and the low marks at school, or that it was a factor in how far off-track I'd gotten. They believe that if you work hard enough, you can overcome anything, which is good at times, but not true for me. With this line of thinking, I end up feeling like a total failure most of the time.

To this day, I don't know if they really understand the impact ADHD has had on my life, but that's okay — I've made my peace with what they're able to understand. It's more important that I find my own way of doing things and don't get too sucked in to their views on what they think will work for me. But one by-product of sharing with them? Now they tell me every time they hear about someone else we know who has ADHD!

CANDACE: I didn't tell anyone about my ADHD for a long time, even though my niece Zoe had a diagnosis. I'm a private person and didn't want anyone judging me for it or seeing me differently. Funny enough, the first person I told was Zoe. She just said, "Cool, me too." That was it. She was an easy first person to share my diagnosis with and, you know, I think it brought us closer. We shared something … something most people can't understand. I told her mother (my sister) too, and she was sort of surprised but not really. I think when your child has ADHD, you start learning about it and looking around at people you know, wondering if they have it, too.

TIM: I'll never forget when I shared my diagnosis with my friend Dave. He didn't believe it and told me there's no way I could have ADHD because of my job and because I've been so successful. He thought people with ADHD would never be able to get through law school. Even though that had been one of my first thoughts when I was diagnosed, his reaction made me really mad.

Here I was sharing something so important about me, that explained so much about what my life had become. It provided a different explanation for the all-nighters at work, my absent parenting, my relationship problems and my drinking habits. Yet, with a few words, Dave took all that away from me. To be fair, he probably thought he was being helpful by saying there isn't anything "wrong" with me. But his response didn't help me with my progress.

That's when I realized I didn't have to tell everyone. I also saw how tenuous my motivation was, so I had to be mindful of that. But a while later, when I told my sister, her response was completely different, much more encouraging. After which, we started to talk about who else in our family may have an ADHD-style brain.

AMY: I remember being really worried about sharing my diagnosis, but when I eventually told my close friend Sarah, she immediately said, "Amy, I kinda already knew that about you." She wasn't surprised at all — didn't question the diagnosis or anything. It was such a relief. She'd known this about me all along and still loved me in spite of my struggles. I was kind of annoyed she'd never pointed it out, but I guess it's not the kind of thing that's easy to tell someone. I had to come to it on my own. Sarah was great at listening while I figured out how having ADHD connected with my loss of my sense of self. She understood my challenges and was supportive of the changes I was working on.

PLOTTING OUT MY TEAM

Look at the diagram below. The inner circle represents the people who are the closest to you. This may include a romantic partner, a roommate, a sibling, a parent or a close friend. The second circle represents close family and friends who are part of your daily dialogue. The outer circle is for people who are in your life a fair amount, but you aren't particularly close with, maybe friends you see at work or socially.

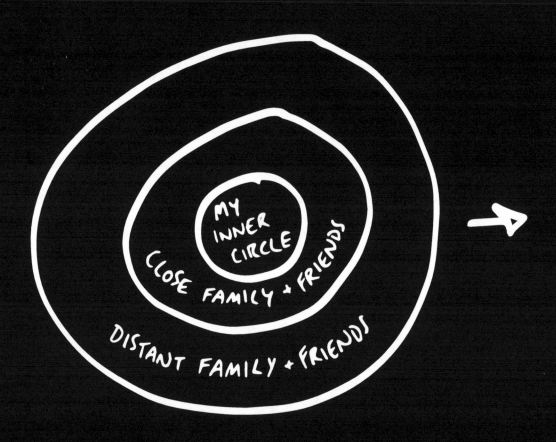

Now plot the people who are part of your life in their respective circles. Put everyone you think is relevant, whether supportive or not. By noting all the main players in your life, you can think about who might have a positive or negative impact on your treatment journey.

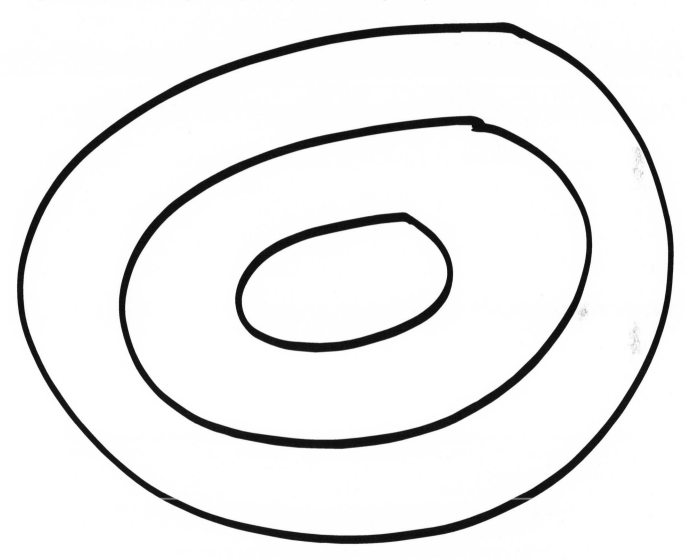

Reflect on who you'd like to have on your support team. Circle the people you want to bring into your journey. Cross out any you'd prefer to keep at arm's length (at least for now). Put a line under any you're not sure about.

SHARING WITH MY TEAM

Learning about having ADHD can offer an opportunity to take stock of your relationships and *also* take responsibility for your past actions and how they may have affected the people who are important to you. When you look at your circle diagram, you may see people who you feel you've let down, with whom you'd like to share your diagnosis. You may also notice individuals who have offered to help you or might be willing to assist you with tasks or challenges moving forward.

Fill in the table below with the team members you circled in the previous section. Jot down what you'd like to share about your journey with ADHD, what type of help you would appreciate from them, as well as what you might be able to offer in return. You obviously have different relationships with your romantic partner, friends, in-laws, family members and work colleagues. The nature of the relationship will influence how an individual can be part of your team and what you want to share.

It may seem tedious to write things out (feel free to use short-form notes), but preparation will help you communicate and get what you need out of these conversations. Not to mention, our clients almost always benefit from taking time to prepare their thoughts.

INNER-CIRCLE MEMBERS

Name	I'd like to communicate ...	I'd like to ask for ...	I'd like to offer ...

MIDDLE-CIRCLE MEMBERS

Name	I'd like to communicate ...	I'd like to ask for ...	I'd like to offer ...

OUTER-CIRCLE MEMBERS

Name	I'd like to communicate ...	I'd like to ask for ...	I'd like to offer ...

RoMANTIC RELATIONSHIPS

Romantic relationships are complicated, but a partner can play a significant role on your team. A key consideration when navigating your romantic relationship is that learning to apologize is a huge skill. And because no one is perfect, it's important that both partners learn it. Being specific about what you're sorry for is more authentic. Apologizing without adding an explanation or a "but" afterward makes an apology even better.

   You might not always be able to control your symptoms, but you can take actions that will compensate for your symptoms in other ways — perhaps by making your partner feel appreciated — in an effort to protect your relationship from the negative patterns that can show up with ADHD.

We've learned a great deal about the interactions of couples with ADHD from Melissa Orlov (check out her books: *The Couple's Guide to Thriving with ADHD* and *The ADHD Effect on Marriage*). One action she refers to is an act of kindness. This is when you do something because it's important to your partner but not necessarily meaningful to you, such as emptying the dishwasher, picking up socks or putting the decorative pillows in the right spots.

Another action we learned from her is a symbolic gesture. This is an action or small gesture that makes your partner feel appreciated, special or loved, such as making them a cup of coffee or tea, offering to watch the kids so they can go to the gym or bringing home small gifts as tokens of appreciation. These kinds of actions can feed back into a romantic relationship by helping buffer it from the stress that can come with ADHD in relationships.

A STORY FROM COACH LAURA:
A TRUE SORRY

Any couple can lose touch with each other's experience. They get blinders on, only focusing on their own thoughts and feelings. When this happens (and it happens all the time), it becomes challenging to hear each other's experience. When a diagnosis of ADHD is in the picture, things get even more complicated.

I once worked with a couple in their late thirties. They were wonderful people — kind, loved each other, wanted to make things better ... but really couldn't hear each other. They were truly stuck, exhausted from the many times they'd lost connection with each other's experiences.

I realized in hearing their dialogue that the husband, who had ADHD, had no ability to say sorry to his wife when his actions affected her. He'd arrive late for something and then go into why he was late and what things had precipitated the lateness. His wife felt unheard. It was all about "the storm" he was going through.

When he saw this effect on his wife and realized he didn't have to be perfect, that he simply had to take responsibility for himself, the weight he carried was lifted. He was able to say "I'm sorry I was late. That meant you felt uncared for and that I was not reliable for you." When he gave her a true sorry, she felt better, he felt better, and they could see each other again.

Loving relationships do not expect perfection of each other. But stepping out of your own experience and realizing how your ADHD affects those around you can help build trust and a shared understanding.

BRAINSTORMING MINI-GESTURES

Jot down some acts of generosity and symbolic gestures you can do to make your partner feel appreciated and loved.

ACTS OF GENEROSITY THAT ARE IMPORTANT TO MY PARTNER	SYMBOLIC GESTURES THAT SHOW MY PARTNER THEY ARE SPECIAL TO ME

WORK RELATIONSHIPS

Our clients often ask us if they should tell their workplace they have ADHD. The answer is tricky. While the academic world encourages students to disclose this information into the post-secondary years, the workplace is more difficult to comment on because roles vary drastically. In some cases, disclosing your strengths and challenges can help you get the right support in place. In other cases, it can put you at risk of being treated differently or judged.

Of course, it's up to you to decide how you want to move forward with getting support in your workplace. By going through the questions on the next two pages, you can assess thoughtfully how you would feel most comfortable going forward.

One thing to point out is that your coworkers (ADHD or not) often benefit from the same tools or approaches you may choose to advocate for. So keep in mind that by setting up better structure, processes and routines in your daily work, you might help others too. You may find that your coworkers appreciate ideas about how to improve the way things are run just as much as you do!

Finding relationships that offer increased social accountability, an audience to help you organize ideas, check-ins to keep you on track with deadlines and meetings, and proofreading support should be mutually beneficial. As you consider how a coworker can help you, reflect on what you can do to support them in return.

Beware though: it can be easy to get interested in other people's duties at work — the novelty of another project can be enticing and distract you from your own tasks! Don't get too immersed in others' work and priorities.

BALANCING WORKPLACE RISKS/REWARDS

We know there's more to be done to make workplaces stigma-free with mental health issues. And although we are passionate about promoting mental health awareness, we encourage you not to be impulsive when making a decision about sharing your personal information with your employer.

As you work through this decision, consider what you have at risk, or what you stand to gain, by telling your workplace. Use these questions to weigh those risks and rewards in determining your approach.

Are there policies in place for mental health support at my workplace?
Are there precedents I could look into?

Do I feel supported by my coworkers and manager?

BALANCING WORKPLACE RISKS/REWARDS CONTINUED

Are my symptoms affecting others and my overall work success?
Or are they more related to my personal well-being?

Are the accommodations I'd benefit from easy enough to put in place
without requiring formal documentation or process?

Will sharing my diagnosis with key people engender my workplace success
and nurture my journey to healing in general?

FAMILY AND FRIENDS

Having family and close friends support you through the ups and downs of ADHD can be the crucial safety net you need when you're struggling. Thinking ahead about the different kinds of support you require and working with the best people on your team for each will put you a step ahead.

For instance, knowing who to call when you haven't met your own expectations and need some encouraging words to stand back up is crucial. Some people may love you no matter what, but they don't know what to say to help you get back on track. In other cases, all you may need is someone who's willing to sit with you as you work through some steps. That accountability partner is ideally someone you've identified before you actually need them.

ADDITIONAL SUPPORT

Your support team can also include people who free up your time and to whom you can delegate tasks — such as a cleaner, organizer or tax accountant — or other experts that will help you execute non-ADHD-friendly tasks.

Many clients will push themselves through certain tasks because they think they *should* be able to get them done. There's that should word again. Beware: under should circumstances, motivation tends to be low and symptoms of ADHD prominent. We support bringing in expertise where you need it so you can spend time and energy on your strengths and interests.

WHO'S ON YOUR TEAM?

Having a team that supports you can reduce loneliness and improve motivation, especially on those tough days. In order to design an authentic team, be open to sharing, willing to let others in and work to be a good friend yourself. Let's hear what happened when our group members opened themselves up to those around them.

JASON: I had to work through a lot of insecurities and independence issues before I finally accepted the idea of working with a private tutor. Plus, I had to try a few before I found somebody who was a good fit. I just needed someone to prompt me, help me get started and organize my ideas — and basically sit there while I did the work. Finding someone with a sense of humor helped. It passed the time and I didn't dread our sessions as much because she brought some fun to them.

CANDACE: I always struggled with getting these long technical reports written by deadline. I'd spend so much time procrastinating and avoiding starting them and then cram them in at the last minute — soooo ADHD. Then a coach I was working with recommended using social accountability.

So I set up a time every week when I'd sit with a coworker and we'd write our reports. We'd often bring snacks or treats, little rewards to make the job more interesting. Getting started is *always* the hardest part. Once that bandage is ripped off, it gets easier. This type of accountability was also great for me from a social perspective — it got me out of my own head.

TIM: When I finally told my boss about my ADHD, assuring her it wouldn't change anything about my billable hours, her response got me thinking. She said they knew I was hardworking and ambitious, but that she didn't want my pride to get in the way of optimizing my work process. She suggested ways to change the format of my week and recommended hiring an admin assistant with top-notch organization skills.

I started figuring out how to delegate more organizational tasks — and being comfortable with that. After all, if someone else can do the same tasks better and faster, I should use my expertise in law for more legal matters. Some things are still really tough, like tracking my billable hours — that's *not* an ADHD-friendly task *at all*.

AMY: When it came to taking care of the house, I was so stuck in my shoulds. "I should be able to clean my own house." But when I finally agreed to get a cleaning service, I was thrilled with the results. I couldn't believe I hadn't tried it sooner! Every once in a while, I still feel a little guilty, but it's freed up my energy and allowed me to turn my mind to other things.

MY POINT PEOPLE

Managing ADHD requires vigilance, and having teammates who understand you is crucial. We cannot emphasize enough how important it is to not go this journey alone.

   Make a shortlist of your point person in each of your environments. As you move forward with them, communicate honestly and openly, so that the relationship never feels one-sided.

	Home	Social	School/work
My point person			
My needs			
What I can offer them			

WHAT HAVE YOU LEARNED IN THIS CHAPTER?
WHAT DO YOU NOW KNOW ABOUT YOU AND YOUR TEAM?

CHAPTER 8

YOU AND YOUR ENVIRONMENT

The right environment is a combination of structure, space, inspiration and accountability. Sorting out what works for you is a personal journey. In our experience, each client is so different. There often isn't a specific pattern. We have clients who feed off the energy of others and go to a crowded coffee shop to "dig in," and individuals who absolutely need to be in a quiet, empty room. Some feel awakened and motivated when pressure kicks in, while others are silenced and immobilized by it.

We're sure about one thing though: your environment can make the ultimate difference between being stuck in disappointed intentions and successfully following through with your goals and dreams — especially when you have ADHD.

This is the last stage in the Finding yourSELF process because it's only once you've done the hard, internal work that you can know how to make changes in your environment. Put simply, you need to know what you need from your environment — but it's not a simple thing.

There's good news though. The steps to addressing your environment are often easier to follow through on because they're usually tangible and structural. This phase can actually be a very satisfying part of your journey. You can imagine yourself saying, "I now know more about what I want and need, and I really want to set up the environment to support this game plan."

WHAT DOES YOUR SUPPORTIVE ENVIRONMENT LOOK LIKE?

Different surroundings can aggravate or mitigate ADHD symptoms and their impact on an individual. Let's hear how our group members created environments they could flourish in.

JASON: I had to come home from university because I was forced to take a leave, and I found myself at home with my parents. That was my lowest point. But on the bright side, it was what led me to finally be open to getting help. It was like my ground zero. I went from doing whatever I wanted with friends, having absolutely no structure, to being with my parents and starting to both need and want help being accountable.

As I built the environment I needed, I had so much to wade through before I could imagine that anything would work for me. One big "aha" moment was about who I was surrounding myself with. I started to hang out more with high school friends, who were into working out. Eventually I got an apartment in the neighborhood where I grew up, so I could walk everywhere and run into people I knew. I had to make sure not to retreat into myself too much. I guess for me, I needed to be around good influences a lot, avoid too much alone time and have a walkable life. That's what I've learned so far anyway.

CANDACE: My apartment pre-diagnosis was as tidy and controlled as a science lab. Everything was carefully curated and fueled by my constant desire for control. As I became more honest with myself about my mental health symptoms, I realized I'd created this immaculate home as a way to protect myself from the chaos I felt inside.

The more I came to terms with this, the more I hated this perfect, sterile-looking space and the story it represented. I needed color in my life. I needed mess. I needed to learn to be okay with a little disruption. My space had become suffocating. That's when I knew I had to change everything around me.

TIM: Changing my environment was first about separating my work life from my home life or, more accurately, actually *having* a home life. I started by leaving my cellphone at the door. Then I changed my work hours. I put more routine into each day with the help of my administrative support. Because I was doing things less last-minute, I could delegate to juniors more often. With help from my group, I was able to meet deadlines and build in more time with my family.

My home became an environment I cared about and wanted to be part of. It wasn't an obligation anymore. I started to belong there. I created a home office, which lets me finish more work after dinner. (Just a bit though!)

AMY: My spaces had been chaotic for as long as I can remember. So when I started to figure out what I needed, I was overwhelmed. My minivan was filled with junk, and my closet looked like a bomb had gone off in it. My personal training files were one big "paplosion" (my term for "paper explosion").

My "lightbulb" moment was realizing I couldn't do this alone and reaching out to Janet, this totally amazing personal organizer. She helped me design spaces I didn't feel overwhelmed by. Getting her help was one of the best decisions I've ever made.

Before this, I had no idea how much that visual stimulation was affecting me. I never went in the home office because I got anxious seeing all the to-do lists I wasn't doing. Once my spaces were comfortable for me, I could cognitively muscle through and put value on my own priorities. I've even been able to maintain my routines. I'll let you in on a secret though: Janet checks in once a month. That recalibration has been huge.

Making customized adjustments to your environment — whether at home, school or work — is a critical part of your long-term success. Sometimes it's about tweaks. Little things, like altering a morning routine or "choosing your battles" as a family, can change everything for the better. Other times, bigger shifts are required, like changing your career or moving to a different city. It's crucial not to feel like your environment is working against the way your brain functions best.

It's not about working harder, it's about working smarter.

To begin the process of figuring out which adjustments might work for you, review your environments, starting with the macro.

Use this as a guide for the following activity.

Time	Home	Work	Play	Community
Morning	*Hectic, crazy, lots of running around*	*Mornings run away from me, have trouble getting started, tend to visit with coworkers*	*Not getting any play, impatient with kids, feel like I'm behind before I even start*	*Feel distant during my commute, tend to be a frustrated and impatient driver*

HOW IS MY "MACRO VIBE" ON A TYPICAL DAY?

By observing your spaces on a typical day, you can assess the roles they play in your life.

Think about where you spend your time, then record the logistics, feelings or activities in each environment. What does each space do or not do for you? Pretend you're an outsider looking in, with fresh eyes and an open mind.

Time	Home	Work	Play	Community
Morning				
Afternoon				
Evening				
Weekend				

THE MICRO

Now dig in to unearth more about the subtle things that motivate you or hold you back.

I get myself out of bed in the morning by ...

My worst days start with ...

I know my day is going to be good when ...

I travel to work/school by ...

I stay on top of healthy eating when ...

I'm most active when ...

My environment calms me if ...

The place where I get the most work done is ...

I feel most at peace when I am ...

I used to think I loved being in ...   but I've learned I'm more productive in ...

The time and place in my day where I feel the least productive is ...

I get overwhelmed by my surroundings when ...

My biggest physical barrier to being productive in my workplace is ...

If I could design something in my home to help with my routine, it would be ...

I'm lying to myself when ...

I feel myself awaken and be motivated when ...

The space where I have created my best work in the past was ...

If I could give my past self one tip about what environment would help, it would be ...

THE MICRO CONTINUED

Sometimes you need to take a little space (from your space) to see where you want to make changes or create new vibes. The goal of this activity is to pull you away from past dialogue with yourself so you can look at your key spaces with fresh eyes. Try not to judge or put too much expectation on yourself. Just go through the exercise and see what comes to fruition.

1. Get your camera out!

2. Take 10 photos of your work and home spaces. These spaces should be chosen by you, but here are a few ideas: car, closet, workspace (home or work), computer's desktop screen, pantry.

3. Categorize these photos based on how they make you feel. You can make your own categories, but here are some recommendations:

— This space is an abyss. I'll get lost trying to organize or fix it.

— I love this space and want to use it more.

— I always think I can be productive here but I'm lying to myself.

— I need help to make this work.

— This space works for me, even if it might look like a tornado to others.

— Something is blocking me here.

— I love this space but always forget about it.

You can also make notes about sounds, textures, visual cues or anything else you notice that could be key in helping you tweak your environments and start a new chapter.

More on the next page ▸

4. Look at "Paring down my goals" activity on page 128 to help you complete the following table. Of the goals you listed, which three are your highest priorities? What environmental factors will block you from following through on these? What changes could you make in your environment that would support you?

Top three goals	Possible blockers	Changes required in my environment	Now tweak

Tip from Coach Laura: When thinking about your environment, remember the importance of leveraging the strengths of your ADHD-style brain. The power of novelty, for example, can be very motivating — implementing your own "outside of the box" ideas ahead of any blockers can be a useful strategy. One idea is to put a sticky note with a motivational quote on your alarm clock or phone that you see before you press the snooze button.

There's an art to having the right amount of routine or structure with lots of space for you to introduce and switch things up. Use your great ideas to stay ahead of any future blockers.

ADHD AND TECHNOLOGY

We could write a whole book on how technology impacts ADHD, but we'll cover a few key thoughts here.

Technology can be extremely distracting. There's more competing stimulation for your brain than ever before. Certainly this can exacerbate time management challenges and increase distractibility. Setting clear rules around your phone usage or your behavior online is crucial. For example, put your phone in the back of the car, so you don't get tempted when you're driving, or turn it off in the evening, so you can get settled for sleep.

That being said, technology can be super helpful with attention issues. For instance, you can set reminders on your phone to stay on track with your priorities. Or use apps for proofreading or managing your time. There's no shortage of useful tools.

The main thing is to be honest with yourself. Continually evaluate and ensure you're using technology to your advantage. So avoid the rabbit hole, but use it as a tool for the right job.

BOOKENDING MY DAYS

Now that you have dug into specific environments, it's time to take a step back, assess your days, as they transition from one environment to the next, and think about the cumulative effect. Seeing how your days are going in the context of your different environments can help you put in necessary structure to stay on top of your daily goals and responsibilities.

How you start and finish your day matters. If you had a great day, it's an opportunity to celebrate and assess how you can make tomorrow also count. If you struggled, it's a chance to regroup (avoid that negative self-talk) and start fresh with a new day. Avoiding black-and-white thinking (today was good or bad) and breaking up your days into small steps (both positive and negative) can help you stay honest about what is going well or getting in the way.

For the next three days, observe what makes your days better (or worse) and record your observations in the following table. Think about which rituals help you stay on track with your goals and help you feel good. Notice when ADHD gets in your way.

Let's see how Tim filled out this sheet as an example...

	Morning *My day begins with:*	Evening *My day closes with:*	Positive steps *What went well? How can I keep this up?*	Blockers *What got in the way? How can I beat these blockers tomorrow?*	My intention for tomorrow
Day 1	- TIME BEING PRESENT W/ MY FAMILY, BEFORE WORK. - COFFEE @ HOME	- WALK AROUND THE BLOCK BEFORE BED, TO SETTLE MY MIND.	- LEFT WORK @ WORK & WAS PRESENT IN THE EVENING @ HOME.	- WAS SLOW TO GET INTO MY WORK IN THE A.M. AT THE OFFICE. - NEED TO START W/ A SMALL TASK (GAIN MOMENTUM)	- KEEP UP W/ HOME ROUTINES. - START WORK @ THE OFFICE W/ ONE SIMPLE TASK.

Tip from Coach Laura: *A tip about mornings (and quitting in general): When your prefrontal cortex and executive functions are not fully engaged and working for you, you're at risk of making a choice that doesn't match with your intentions. It can be easier to give up on a goal like waking up early to go for a run or get to a class. Of course, this is true for everyone, but having ADHD can put you at greater risk of giving up on something in the moment.*

To help you stay accountable, put as many things in place ahead of time. Even recording a message as your alarm can work — something like "Beat ADHD and just get outside, even for six minutes, even if it's later than you thought, start now."

And don't let ADHD trick you. If you planned to go for a run in the morning, start by getting outside. If you really don't want to run, walk around the block. Don't let that pesky ADHD bird hold you back from doing what you really want.

| | Morning | Evening | Positive steps | Blockers | My intention for tomorrow |
	My day begins with:	*My day closes with:*	*What went well? How can I keep this up?*	*What got in the way? How can I beat these blockers tomorrow?*	
Day 1					
Day 2					
Day 3					

There's no way around it: environment is so key to beating ADHD. Many of our clients have successfully sustained their treatment by changing their environment. Students have realized that, to get their studying done, they need to find a secret place in the library and lock themselves in. Adults have made *huge* changes. Even moving to the country to be in a more peaceful place, or to the city — and a smaller place — to take away a commute. It's often a deeply personal process to assess what you need out of your space to do what you want and need to do.

The one message that's remained true is this:

> ***Once you find the right environment, stay dedicated to these habits.***

The number one thing we hear from clients who return for coaching because they're struggling after having been successful for a long time is that they've stopped staying true to what they know works for them.

Don't let your ADHD bird tell you that you don't need that walk or that the commute will be fine this time. Wake up every day conquering that ADHD bird by setting up the environment that works best for you.

WHAT HAVE YOU LEARNED IN THIS CHAPTER?
WHAT DO YOU NOW KNOW ABOUT YOU AND YOUR ENVIRONMENT?

CHAPTER 9

MEDICAL CONSIDERATIONS AND IDEAS

BY DR. AINSLIE GRAY

Not everyone who has an ADHD diagnosis needs to add medication to their treatment regimen. This is a choice you make with your medical team. Every individual with ADHD has ownership to explore their own journey. As you consider your options, you should feel like an empowered collaborator. Never feel pressured to take medication, and always trust your own personal health barometer.

In this chapter, I share key considerations in the area of medical alternatives. We hope the Finding yourSELF process has allowed you to gain important and unique self-awareness and that you feel connected with your wants and needs as you consider additional medical supports.

This chapter is not an official step in the Finding yourSELF process, but presents some general themes you may find helpful. This information does not constitute prescriptive medical advice. Please talk to your medical team about what would be best for you.

If you're not interested in exploring medication as an option, feel free to skip this chapter.

BEGINNING YOUR JOURNEY

As a primary care physician with a focused mental health practice for over 20 years, I've had the opportunity and honor to witness the truly life-changing role the use of medication, in combination with coaching and therapy, can have on my patients' lives. The success of treatment can be powerful.

Let me begin by telling you about Alison. She's a middle-aged woman who came to Springboard Clinic requesting support for her 12-year-old daughter. By observing and learning about her daughter's ADHD diagnosis, Alison soon realized that her own childhood diagnosis of ADHD had never completely resolved and was now interfering with her adult life.

Alison's experience of being given immediate-release stimulant medication on a regimen of four-hour doses was something she would never want for her child. The negative impact of the labeling and stigma she experienced was profound. However, Alison noticed that the success of her child's coaching was being compromised by her inability to stay engaged with her coach, teachers and family members, even during treatment sessions. An impasse had been reached.

When Alison and her daughter heard that there are now longer-acting medicines that provide a once-daily dosage, they were willing to try pharmaceutical intervention. These newer medications offer an extended and smoother experience so that you "feel more like yourself."

This type of medication support allowed her to control her executive functions and feel like she could finally follow through when she wanted to. Neither could have been more thrilled. Starting with a low dose and gradually increasing in order to monitor both the support and side effects proved to be the secret of their success.

Too often, negative memories, experiences and media messages create anxiety and apprehension about seeking medical support and considering medication for ADHD. Occasionally, people with ADHD are referred to in negative or derogatory ways, such as "lazy," "unmotivated" or "out of control." As an experienced medical professional in the field, I know these labels are not only untrue, but can also have a negative impact on patients' willingness to seek help. It's important that we share stories of hope and success and that we motivate individuals to get support for their struggles.

This chapter should answer some of your questions and reduce concerns regarding the use of medication. The following questions are common to the experience of many patients and physicians. I hope they'll be helpful as you continue your journey of self-discovery. When patients are empowered by knowledge and success, ongoing compliance becomes much higher.

WHAT IS MEDICATION FOR ADHD?

The medications that support ADHD change the neurotransmitters in your brain's prefrontal cortex, allowing your executive functions to work more optimally.

In essence, this part of the brain acts like an orchestra conductor, to organize and coordinate the brain's activity. When an individual has ADHD, their prefrontal cortex experiences inconsistent levels of available neurotransmitters, which are the chemicals that carry messages among brain cells. This means the brain's conductor "falls asleep on the job." You can imagine what the orchestra sounds like when the conductor is not focused!

Put simply, ADHD medications help engage your brain to manage projects and stay engaged. They work so you can stay in control of starting tasks, staying on tasks, blocking out distractions, using working memory and regulating your emotions.

Stimulants are the most common medications for ADHD. There are two main types — amphetamines and methylphenidate — which influence the amount and availability of neurotransmitters to support ADHD signs and symptoms.

"Non-stimulants" may also be used. Their action can be more subtle, by reducing anxiety and helping with emotional regulation. For people with additional traits or diagnoses, such as autistic spectrum characteristics, tics, depression or anxiety, it may be beneficial to combine both stimulant and non-stimulant medications to provide 24-hour focusing support.

One young woman confided in our team that she'd never been able to read a book cover to cover. She shared that the non-stimulant medication helped motivate her to pick up a book, and the stimulant medication provided acuity and focus to actually read it. This realization was both enlightening and supportive to her as she learned how to make medication work for her own lifestyle choices. Medication should feel like a "helper," allowing you to become closer to your true self and follow through more consistently with your intentions.

HOW HAS ADHD MEDICATION CHANGED AND IMPROVED?

Although stimulant medication was first approved for medical use in 1956, it was in the early 1990s that ADHD medications became more commercially available. At that time, there were very few medication options, and they were what is now referred to as immediate-release preparations. This means that the full dosage of the medication is released immediately after it's taken. While these types of medications may allow for a burst of support to get your day started, their supportive effects tend to be relatively short-lasting.

Through extensive research and clinical experience, ADHD medications have evolved to include longer-lasting, extended-release options. Their development has also increased their safety and improved access of support for all ages.

IF I START USING MEDICATION, DO I HAVE TO STAY ON IT FOREVER?

No. Medication is designed to act as a supportive aid in your ADHD journey. The role it plays is unique to each individual. Some people benefit from long-term medication use to keep them on track with their goals. Some use medication for only a short time to help get them started on their journey. Still others feel that medication is not a necessary or desired component to their treatment at all.

The choice to start and stop is yours, with your medical team's recommendations — just make sure you stay true to yourself.

WILL I BECOME DEPENDENT ON THE MEDICATION?

Potentially, but not in the way you might think. People choose to take daily stimulant medication because it improves the management of their ADHD signs and symptoms. In that sense, if the medication is working with minimal side effects, it may be something you want to use long-term.

That being said, the support from stimulant medication has often worn off by the end of the day. Dr. Annick Vincent, a well-known Canadian psychiatrist, likens taking stimulant medication to wearing eyeglasses. Once there's no further support from the stimulant medication, it's like the glasses have been removed ... until you take the medication again.

Because the effects of stimulant medication lapse at the end of the day, you can usually choose to stop taking it at any time (upon your physician's advice). There's no physical dependence on the medication, but many people feel better by taking it daily because their ADHD becomes less impairing. The "dependence" comes from recognizing the positive effects of pharmaceutical intervention with its use.

Non-stimulant medications are another story. Because they provide ongoing 24-hour support, they must be taken consistently with daily compliance and should not be terminated abruptly. It is imperative that you work with your physician closely to determine whether this medication is supportive, and to establish a slow process if you choose to discontinue.

Now, let me tell you about Jack. He's a professionally educated, successful corporate banker. When he came to see our team, he was frustrated with time management, struggled with productivity and was feeling anxious in both his work and home environments. Jack required extra time to complete his tasks and depended on the feeling of urgency with last-minute deadlines to motivate him. This intense way of trying to cope was unsatisfactory and he subsequently turned to daily substance use.

After a diagnosis of ADHD, Jack developed effective strategies to manage his ADHD through coaching and therapy, he also realized that daily medication use provided what he needed to follow through and to manage his life in a more balanced way. This treatment combination made his days feel more successful, which reduced and finally eliminated his substance abuse. The support provided by the medication allowed Jack to no longer be dependent on other, less effective coping mechanisms.

WHAT ARE SOME MEDICATION SIDE EFFECTS I MAY EXPERIENCE?

Side effects may include loss of appetite, sleep interference and mood variability. Many things can be done to avoid or reduce these concerns, including varying the type of medication, dose and time at which it is taken.

Pay attention to how your body feels while on the medication. Although side effects may be present, they should never be intolerable. If you don't feel supported, ask your healthcare provider for a lower or higher dose or a different medication. Finding the right medication is often a trial-and-error process. Don't lose hope if the first couple of doses or types of medication don't work well.

Always consult your physician as you explore alternatives.

WHAT ARE THE MOST IMPORTANT THINGS TO REMEMBER WHILE TAKING MEDICATION?

- Make healthy choices with what you eat and drink. Medication does not replace a balanced lifestyle.

- Eat a good breakfast. This should include protein to support optimal nutrition throughout the day, especially when a reduced appetite may limit interest in eating.

- Drink at least 6 to 8 glasses of water a day.

- Avoid caffeine use. Caffeine is also a stimulant and, when used in combination with a stimulant or other medication, may cause you to feel anxious. Track any uncomfortable feelings, noting the timing and amount of your caffeine intake.

- To set up a consistent regimen of care, take your medication early in the morning. Doing so can help you get a good start to your day and mitigate potential sleep issues. If you are employed with shift work, you may need to make accommodations.

- Exercise at least 20 minutes a day, ideally before breakfast. Regular daily exercise may enable you to reduce the dose of the stimulant, as it also supports your prefrontal cortex along with your medication.

- Discontinue nicotine use (it's also a stimulant).

- Stop the use of screens (television, computers and video games) at least one hour before bed. The screen's light may interfere with your production of melatonin, the hormone produced by the brain to prepare for sleep.

WHAT WAS YOUR EXPERIENCE WITH ADHD MEDICATION?

Just as each person's journey with ADHD is unique and personal, so too is their experience with and decision to use or not use medication. Let's see how our group members approached the issue of medical intervention.

JASON: At first, medication wasn't something I wanted on board. I had enough things going on with the eating and the drinking, and thought that if I took medication to focus, I wouldn't even know how to use this focus. I was home from school and not really up to anything. So I chose to not go that way.

Over time though, as I got through a bunch of the emotional stuff and realized I wanted to go back to school, I decided to try stimulant medication. I have to say, I'm glad I didn't rush into it, but it really does help me stay on track. Each morning, I take a low dose of stimulant medication, and it helps me get through my work and keep up with my routines. I don't think I'll take it forever, but, for now, it's helping me get through this academic chapter.

CANDACE: I chose not to go the medical route. I felt that my process was manageable without adding a pharmaceutical solution. Maybe I'll consider looking into it down the road, but so far I've made great progress through my cognitive changes alone.

I look at it this way: I can focus well when I'm into something, so I don't really need the meds for that. If anything, I guess it would be to reduce anxiety, but I've made such huge strides through my own coaching that, unless things get worse or I stop making progress, I think I'll go without. It feels right for me.

TIM: ADHD medication has made a crucial difference for me — in fact, it's been life-altering. Agreeing to take it was a big hurdle though. It felt like admitting there was something "wrong or different" about me. I was kind of freaked out about it, to be honest. But I'm so glad I decided to be open-minded: it's helped me come to terms with how inefficient I was and how distant I was from family and friends, too. I'm now able to follow through on the stuff I want. On a daily basis, it helps me keep up with my goals, and stay present.

AMY: I did try medication and it did help. It was sort of a relief to understand better and get a feel for what I'm aiming for with controlling my focus. But I decided I didn't want to stay on it — it didn't feel right for me. Maybe if I were going back to school or doing something that required me to sit still and get things done, I'd think about it again. But I've been able to manage my symptoms through daily physical activity, changes in my lifestyle, coaching, as well the support from my professional organizer. I understand myself better, so I can sort of push through. So, for now, I'm doing okay. I feel pretty proud I can say that aloud. From here, I'll just keep reassessing over time.

WHAT HAVE YOU LEARNED IN THIS CHAPTER?
HOW DO YOU WANT TO APPROACH MEDICAL TREATMENT FOR YOURSELF?

A FINAL WORD

Having a brain difference or mental health diagnosis is never easy. In order to cope and even thrive, it takes hard work, every day. Actually, let's say that differently: it takes strategic work, every day. Many of our clients return to the Finding yourSELF process to reassess a game plan when new challenges or life transitions test their coping skills.

As you take on your next challenges, keep these messages in mind:

Keep your defenses down. Being defensive about your symptoms tends to create an emotional response that can hold you back. Remember, if you have gone through the Finding yourSELF process carefully, you know your natural strengths and where you struggle. When you experience symptoms, take a breath, take ownership of what happened, realize the impact it had on others and look to solve.

At all costs, try to avoid the cycle of being "upset about being upset." Laugh when it's funny and apologize when you've affected others. Then, do what you do best: creatively problem-solve through it so you can get back on track.

Keep talking with your team. Let your people in on your journey. What's going well, where you're making headway and where you need more support or structure. Don't wait until you've really fallen behind and are overwhelmed by what needs to be done. For example, let's say you're having trouble finishing your paperwork on time. Don't wait until you have two months of lagging paperwork. Talk about it now. Having your point person literally sit beside you while you go through it the first time can help you assess those blockers and get back on track.

Take responsibility for yourself and your actions. If you have successfully gone through the Finding yourSELF program, you know about how your brain works. You know what you need to do and have strategies for helping you stay on track. Keep using these. If things are going more smoothly, don't think you can stop thinking about ADHD. Always keep it there, always be active in this process. Every day, stop, take a breath and ask yourself, "Who's in charge? Me or ADHD?"

Trust your gut. This means you first have to listen to yourself. Your voice is powerful. Your inner thoughts will drive you to make the decisions you know you're capable of — they'll also hold you back if you start to let ADHD be in charge. Deep down, you know what you need, so keep talking back to that ADHD bird. Don't let the voice that drives a cycle of disappointment come back and nag at you. Follow what you know to be the right journey.

Wake up each day in charge. Approach next steps with "a one day at a time" vision and make each day count. Don't wait for your morning to hit you and become reactive to what comes at you. Plan your day the night before. Establish a structure that ensures you'll start the morning on the right foot. Go for a run. Have a spot for your keys.

Don't be afraid to ask for help. There's no need to go it alone — professionals are here to support you along your journey. If you're struggling, reach out to and connect with your physician, work with a coach or therapist, join a support group or talk with a supportive friend.

Remember, passion is a great motivator. Wherever possible, follow your passions. Figure out what things make you tick naturally and use them to stay motivated and productive. Realize that you'll be more successful if you care deeply about what you're doing, and you'll feel more fulfilled, too. Whatever you do, don't be afraid to think outside the box. Life is not black or white. Quite the opposite actually. And you were never going to think inside the box in the first place.

Above all, be kind to yourself. In taking on the voices of critics (including your own doubts), you fuel the symptoms that hold you back. By believing that you have in you the intention, the talent, the skills and the ability to beat ADHD, you'll keep your focus on what will help you be the person you want to be. Accept you for you, ADHD for ADHD, remember that you are not your ADHD — and then be kind and believe.

We believe in you. We've heard story after story of hope. We love working in the field of ADHD precisely for that reason. We truly feel that ADHD doesn't have to hold you back, and we wish you the best as you move forward. We know that your story too can be one of inspiration.

We hope you've explored the activities, ideas and stories, and found this workbook helpful. We also hope you've made this experience yours by skipping over what doesn't resonate and circling what feels relevant. As you move through your journey, reread parts or explore your answers again — chances are, they will change as you evolve.

Finally, we encourage you to go forward feeling more aware of yourself and your next steps and knowing that you have a whole community rooting for you. Share your story, connect with others in the same boat and join us in delivering a message of hope.

ABOVE ALL, BE KIND TO YOURSELF.

DID YOU LOVE *MAY WE HAVE YOUR ATTENTION PLEASE?*

SHARE YOUR PRAISE:

Did this book help you? Did it offer a new understanding of adult ADHD? If so, we'd warmly welcome a review, shared through your favorite online retailer. A few minutes of your time would mean the world to us, and your review (anonymous or with your name) could help others to find our book, buy a copy and hopefully benefit as you have.

PLACE A BULK ORDER:

Would you like to share this book with a group and order 20 (or more) copies? Please drop us a line. We can offer bulk discounts for orders within North America. Write to info@springboardclinic.com.

We'd love to hear from you!

For more tips, resources and stories or to explore our services, visit **springboardclinic.com** We are constantly evolving and always keen to take on new adventures in ADHD support. Don't be a stranger!

Follow us:

 @springboardclinic

 /SpringboardClinic

 @springboardadhd